C000145183

About this Learning Guide

Shmoop Will Make You a Better Lover*
*of Literature, History, Poetry, Life...

Our lively learning guides are written by experts and educators who want to show your brain a good time. Shmoop writers come primarily from Ph.D. programs at top universities, including Stanford, Harvard, and UC Berkeley.

Want more Shmoop? We cover literature, poetry, bestsellers, music, US history, civics, biographies (and the list keeps growing). Drop by our website to see the latest.

www.shmoop.com

Table of Contents

Introduction

In a Nutshell

Othello is a tragedy written by William Shakespeare around 1603. The play tells the story of a powerful general of the Venetian army, Othello, whose life and marriage are ruined by a conniving, deceitful, and envious soldier, Iago.

Othello is possibly the most famous literary exploration of the warping powers of jealousy and suspicion. At the same time, it's among the earliest literary works dealing with race and racism. Othello, undeniably heroic even if ultimately flawed, is the most prominent black protagonist in early Western literature. Othello faces constant racism from other characters, especially when he marries Desdemona, a privileged white woman whose father disapproves of the union.

The play's performance history has been marked by racism. To see a real black man and a white woman kiss onstage was seen as so unacceptable to many viewers that even in early twentieth century America, Othello had to be played by a white man in blackface. When Paul Robeson, a black American and the son of a slave, played Othello on Broadway in the 1940s, the performances electrified a still segregated nation.

Why Should I Care?

Othello's treatment of race and sexuality makes its one of Shakespeare's most relevant and controversial plays. For some, the play's portrayal of a black man who marries and then brutally murders a white woman in a fit of rage and jealousy makes *Othello* a racist play. For these critics, Shakespeare seems to endorse a xenophobic (anti-foreigner) attitude that was pretty common throughout England and other parts of Europe. After all, they say, the play is full of characters that express a blatant hatred of black men and foreigners, and these characters often refer to Othello as "thick-lips," the "devil," and the "old black ram" who supposedly contaminates his white wife with his hyper-sexuality. Not only that, but Othello enacts a racist stereotype (that says black men are "savage") when he strangles his wife on her bed.

Yet, for other critics, neither the action in the play nor the characters' racist attitudes makes the play (or Shakespeare) racist. For some, *Othello* is a play that portrays racism in a way that provokes the audience into *re*thinking its ideas and attitudes about race. Many critics argue that Shakespeare's play asks us to consider the tragedy of how Othello absorbs and internalizes the dominant racist attitudes that surround him. The idea is that *Othello* is a study of what happens when a society tells a man over and over and over again that he is violent, savage, contaminating, and to be feared. In the case of Othello, the character begins to believe it's all true and acts out a racist stereotype – that of a "savage" killer.

If you're thinking that all of this is irrelevant in a world where the first black man (that would be Barack Obama) has been elected to the U.S. presidency, then you might want to consider this: In October, 2009, a white Justice of the Peace in Louisiana refused to marry an interracial couple (source). Hmm. It seems like *Othello* is worth checking out, wouldn't you say?

Summary

Book Summary

We start out in Venice, Italy, land of love and water. We meet two guys early on: Iago and Roderigo. Iago, who's been taking money from Roderigo in some sort of "arrangement," is upset at "the Moor," a.k.a. Othello, our tragic hero. Othello is a general in the Venetian army, and he just chose another man, Cassio, to be his lieutenant. This angers Iago, who wanted the position for himself.

Iago and Roderigo decide to get back at Othello by making a nighttime visit to Brabantio, the father of Desdemona (a.k.a. the woman Othello has recently eloped with). When Iago and Roderigo tattle on Othello for marrying Desdemona without her father's permission, Brabantio rushes to his daughter's room and discovers that she is missing. According to the angry father, this must mean that "the Moor" somehow "tricked" his daughter into whatever the two of them are doing together.

Cut to Othello in the next day or so, who's hanging out with Iago and talking about his , new wife, Desdemona. Trouble is brewing since Brabantio is a senator and therefore rather influential. It's clear that he'll try to split the pair up. But Othello isn't worried. Since he's legendary in the Venetian military, he believes his service record will get him through just fine. He adds that he really loves Desdemona, too.

The conversation is interrupted by Michael Cassio (the guy who got the lieutenant position over Iago), who says the Duke of Venice needs to see Othello right away, because there's some military action going down in Cyprus. Before everyone can peacefully exit, Brabantio shows up with Roderigo and various henchmen, ready to kill Othello or at least maim him severely for having the audacity to marry his daughter. Looks like everyone is off to see the Duke and settle the matter.

Once we get to the Duke, Othello speaks in his defense: he says Desdemona was an equal participant in their courting, and there was no trickery involved. They're now very much in love and married. Our woman in question, i.e. Desdemona, finally arrives and confirms the whole story. At this, the Duke tells Brabantio to stop whining and sends Othello to fight the battle in Cyprus. Desdemona states that she'll come along, as do Iago, his wife Emilia, Cassio, and Roderigo.

Iago and Roderigo have a little conversation during which Roderigo complains about being lovesick for Desdemona, and Iago says he'll get them together as soon as they bring down Othello. Once alone, Iago reveals a rumor that Othello was having sex with Iago's wife, Emilia. (The rumor is totally untrue and it's not even clear that Iago believes it.) To get revenge, he'll take out Cassio and Othello by convincing Othello that Cassio is having sex with Othello's wife, Desdemona.

So our cast of characters gets transported to Cyprus, where instead of battle there's just a big party (long story, read your play for the details). We note that Cassio is a ladies man, especially around Emilia. While on watch together, Iago gets Cassio drunk and orchestrates a fight between him and Roderigo.

Othello intervenes and fires Cassio for being belligerently drunk instead of doing his job. Iago then convinces Cassio that he should ask Desdemona to tell Othello to give him back his job. Once alone, Iago schemes more about how he's going to convince Othello that Desdemona is having an affair with Cassio.

Cassio talks to Desdemona and she agrees to try to convince her husband to give Cassio his job back. As Othello is seen approaching, Cassio slinks off, not wanting to have an awkward moment with the guy that just fired him. Iago (entering with Othello) notes how suspicious it is that Cassio hurried off like that. Once the two men are alone, Iago plants (and massively fertilizes) the seed of suspicion. Cassio, he hints, is having an affair with Desdemona. He warns Othello to keep his eye out for anything suspicious, like Desdemona talking about Cassio all the time and pleading for his job back.

Othello is so upset he gets physically ill. Once Desdemona is back, she tries to bandage his head playfully with the "special handkerchief" Othello once gave her, a symbol of their undying love, an heirloom from his dead mother, and eventually the cause of a whole lot of trouble – which is why we later call it "the handkerchief of death."

To make a long story short, Emilia steals the handkerchief for her husband Iago, whom we learn has asked for it repeatedly in the past. Iago plants the handkerchief of death in Cassio's room. Othello enters, and Iago furthers Othello's suspicions with the aid of various outright lies. When Othello learns about the handkerchief, he decides that Desdemona is cheating on him, and because of that, she has to die.

The next scene brings us to Othello arguing with Desdemona while Emilia watches. He wants to know where the handkerchief is and Desdemona, oblivious, wants to talk about Cassio. Fighting ensues.

Shortly afterwards, we meet Bianca, a prostitute who's in love with Cassio. Cassio gives her the handkerchief he got from Iago, and swears it's not a love token from another woman. Some time later, Iago sets up a conversation between himself and Cassio, in which he gets Cassio to speak provocatively about Bianca. According to Iago's plan, somehow Othello, hiding and listening in, will think Cassio's speaking of Desdemona. So while Cassio is saying, "Yeah, I gave it to her good," Othello is thinking, "I'm going to kill that guy."

To make matters even worse, Bianca storms in and throws the special handkerchief in Cassio's face, having discovered that it indeed belonged to another woman. She storms out, with Cassio following behind her. Othello rages for a bit, and Iago advises that he strangle Desdemona. The next time the couple interacts, Othello hits her in the face (in front of a messenger from Venice telling him he has to go back home). Shortly after that, Othello yells at his wife, calling her a "whore," a "strumpet," and lots of other hurtful names. Filled with jealousy and indignation, he eventually resolves to kill his wife.

Back on the other manipulation front, Roderigo is getting tired of Iago taking all his money and not delivering the goods (i.e., Desdemona), as promised. Iago tells him to cool his jets, and also to kill Cassio when the opportunity arises, which, according to Iago, will happen that night between midnight and 1:00 AM.

Meanwhile, Desdemona and Emilia are talking together, and Desdemona begins to act strangely, foreshadow her own death. She sings of it, too. Emilia, meanwhile, defends the act of cheating on one's spouse, especially if there's a good reason for it.

Iago and Roderigo hang out, waiting for Cassio. Roderigo tries to stab Cassio, fails, gets stabbed himself, and looks to be in trouble until Iago sneaks up and stabs Cassio in the leg. Two Venetian gentlemen run in at the sound of Cassio's screaming. Iago pretends he just stumbled in himself, declares Roderigo to be the assailant, and stabs Roderigo to death before the man can claim otherwise. Bianca runs in and screams a bit, and Iago tries to pin the mess on her. Emilia enters and Iago weaves her a lying tale. He instructs her to tell Othello and his wife about the news.

Othello, meanwhile, kills Desdemona, just as Emilia enters the room. In this moment of confusion, Emilia reports (incorrectly) to Othello that Cassio killed Roderigo. Othello is furious to find that Cassio is still alive, as that was definitely not the plan. Emilia finally puts two and two together and realizes her own husband is the cause of everyone's tragedy.

As people pour into the room, Emilia outs Iago for being a rat. Iago promptly stabs his wife, but not so promptly that the truth can't come out first. Othello demands to know why Iago ruined his entire life, but Iago refuses to give him (and us) a good reason. The Venetian gentlemen decide to take Othello back to Venice to face his punishment for killing his wife, and Cassio inherits Othello's post in Cyprus. Othello, overwhelmed by grief, decides to end his life rather than live without Desdemona.

Act 1, Scene 1

- We meet Roderigo and Iago, having a spat on a street in Venice, Italy. We, the audience, have just walked in on the conversation, so we're not exactly clear about why they're fighting, yet. We learn that Roderigo has been doling out cash to Iago, and that he's now upset about some news Iago has delivered. Roderigo, referring to this news, says, "I thought you hated him!" and Iago says, "Of course, I hate him!" and we're asking, "Who the heck are you guys talking about?" and Shakespeare says, "In good time, grasshoppers."
- Iago explains his reason to hate this "him." Iago got three of Venice's VIPs to advocate to "him," asking "him" to make Iago a lieutenant. Iago knows he's worthy of the position, if he does say so himself, but the mystery "man" apparently rebuffed the VIPs and said he'd already chosen a lieutenant, another guy named Michael Cassio.
- Iago is displeased, especially because this Cassio is a numbers guy, a great arithmetician who has no knowledge of battle except for what he's read. Iago believes that Cassio will be useless in war.

- Thus, Iago is peeved that he's basically still an ancient (or ensign, meaning the lowly ranked guy who carries the flag of an army in war) instead of second-in-command to the Moor, Othello. So now we've learned that the "him" is a black man who is a general in the Venetian army. Just to be clear, Othello is the one who passed Iago over for the lieutenant position. (FYI: throughout this entire first scene, Othello is only referred to as "the Moor" and never by personal name. In keeping with the original text, we'll refer to Othello as "the Moor" for this first scene.)
- Iago complains more that people gain advancement because they're smart and loved, instead of reasons of seniority. He's bitter. Still, Iago promises he'll get his revenge: he'll pretend to love the Moor and do service to him, but he plans to betray this Moor the first chance he gets. Iago declares, "I am not what I am," which is a perfect introduction to this treacherous, lying jerk-o-saur.
- After Roderigo makes some nasty racial comments about the Moor, Iago suggests that they go now to "her father" and make a big scene at his place. Roderigo and Iago thus show up under the sleeping Brabantio's window, making quite the ruckus. They proclaim that Brabantio should watch out for thieves – and for his daughter.
- Brabantio comes to the window in a fury, ready to shoo off what sounds like drunken idiots making noise under his window while he's trying to sleep. Iago, hidden by the night, proclaims that Brabantio's heart should be broken, as half of his soul is stolen. Iago declares to him that "an old black ram is tupping your white ewe."
- Roderigo realizes that Brabantio doesn't recognize his voice, so he declares it's him, Roderigo. Brabantio then clues in and tells him to get lost. He's told Roderigo before that his daughter has no interest in marrying him, so would the drunken, fat Roderigo please leave his window and stop stalking his daughter?
- Roderigo and the hidden Iago continue to mock Brabantio about his daughter. They yell that they might be drunk, but they have news! Even as the men are hollering out of the windows, they say that Brabantio's daughter is being promiscuous with the Moor.
- Roderigo insists that Brabantio's daughter has run off to the Moor's bed, and he tells Brabantio to check and see whether his daughter is actually in her room, if he doesn't believe him.
- As Brabantio sets off to see if his daughter is safe in her bed, Iago tells Roderigo that he'll be leaving now. It won't look good if he (Iago) is found with Roderigo, plotting the Moor's demise, when he's supposed to be on the Moor's side.
- Iago notes that while the state may not like the Moor's behavior, the state can't afford to get rid of him right now. The state has recently entered into war in Cyprus, and no one can rival Othello as a general. Basically, they need him, even if they don't like him personally.
- Iago tells Roderigo that, at the moment, he's got to see the Moor, but he'll meet Roderigo later at this pub, the Sagitarry, where he'll be with the Moor.
- After Iago has left, Brabantio returns in a rage. His daughter is indeed gone. Brabantio wonders aloud whether the girl has married the Moor.
- Roderigo confirms the two are likely married, and Brabantio declares that men should trust their daughters' actions and not what their daughters say.
- Brabantio then insists that the Moor must've tricked his daughter, enchanting the girl to fall in love with him. In frustration, Brabantio says he wishes Roderigo had married his daughter after all. Roderigo then graciously agrees to go with Brabantio on a hunt to find this wayward girl. They'll even get the whole neighborhood involved.

Act 1, Scene 2

- Othello, the Moor, is with Iago on another street in Venice. Iago is going on about how he's murdered a lot of people, but he really doesn't like to do it, because he's such an upstanding guy. Still, he tells Othello, he had a hard time not killing Brabantio, mostly because of the awful things he was saying about Othello. (Iago conveniently leaves out that he's the one who inspired Brabantio to trash-talk Othello in the first place. Oh, the treachery!)
- Othello is calm, and says it's a good thing Iago didn't kill his father-in-law. Iago prattles on, asking if Othello's marriage is "fast" and "secure." It seems Iago is asking whether Othello's had sex with Desdemona yet, as marriages that had yet to be consummated (or sealed by having sex) could still be annulled. (We can safely assume that Desdemona is Brabantio's daughter.)
- Iago is wagging in the Moor's ear that Brabantio is a Senator, and one who is so powerfully persuasive that he's almost twice as influential as the Duke of Venice. Iago is sure that Brabantio will try to have his daughter and Othello divorced, or otherwise raise hell for poor Othello.
- Othello isn't going to stress about it. In fact, he's certain his record as a general and his service to Venice will stand up against any of Brabantio's complaints in Venice's eyes. Further, Othello says he simply loves Desdemona; he wouldn't have given up his freedom as a bachelor for anything less.
- Their conversation is interrupted by some commotion. Iago assumes it's the warring Brabantio, and he encourages Othello to run off and hide, but Othello decides to stand and face his father-in-law like a man. Actually, the interruption is not the father-in-law mob at all, but Michael Cassio (the great arithmetician, and Othello's second-in-command) with many other officers.
- Cassio brings the grave news that a dozen messengers have been coming with growing news of a war from Cyprus. The Duke of Venice and the Senate have been searching for Othello, who wasn't at his house. The Duke demands Othello's presence to deal with this matter immediately, even though it's the middle of the night.
- Othello rushes off, leaving Cassio with Iago and just enough time for Iago to tell Cassio that the reason Othello wasn't around is that he was busy stealing away and getting married. Before Cassio can hear that Othello's new wife is Brabantio's daughter, Desdemona, Othello returns to get Cassio to go with him.
- Just then, their exit is cut off by Brabantio, who's finally arrived with Roderigo and officers in tow. They're here to raise a riot against Othello. Swords are lifted all around. Othello and Brabantio's men plan to go at it with one another, but Othello stops them to ask what exactly Brabantio thinks he's doing. Brabantio explains that he's just come to clear up the little matter of Othello bewitching and stealing his daughter.
- Brabantio says his daughter was so anti-marriage prior to meeting Othello that she wouldn't marry even the wealthiest boys in the kingdom. Brabantio is sure his daughter's sudden marriage to Othello is the result of witchcraft, and he'd like to have Othello locked up for practicing black magic.
- Othello, still calm, says even if he wanted to go to prison, it would only get Brabantio in

trouble. The Duke is waiting to hear from Othello about this business with Cyprus, and would be none-too-happy if his favorite general was locked up for marriage-related reasons.

- Brabantio insists that his matter is important, too, regardless of what's keeping the Duke up at this hour. If the Duke or any of the other men of state knew a senator's daughter was out cavorting with a Moor and were comfortable with it, then all of Venice might have "bond-slaves and pagans" for their representatives – which is not a nice thing to say about Othello.

Act 1, Scene 3

- The Duke and assorted senators of Venice are dealing with the impending war with the Turks over Cyprus, an island in the Mediterranean. The men compare conflicting reports of a Turkish fleet approaching the island, but are interrupted by a messenger, who says that, actually, the Turkish fleet is headed to Rhodes (yet another island, this one in between Greece and Cyprus).
- After much quibbling, the men realize that the Turkish fleet sent to Rhodes was only a decoy, as Cyprus is more strategically important to the enemy. The governor of Cyprus, Montano, has sent a message from his location in Florence to confirm that his city is soon to be under siege: the Turks, with a fleet of 30 ships, really are headed for Cyprus, and he needs help from Venice – right now.
- Brabantio enters the scene with Othello, Cassio, Iago, Roderigo, and a bevy of other officers. The Duke is quick to dispatch Othello to fight the Ottomans, but Brabantio pipes up. He says he hasn't come on matters of state, but rather because his daughter's been stolen.
- The Duke says this is awful news, ignoring that this is probably not as awful as the fact that Cyprus is about to be pulverized by the Turks. Still, the Duke promises that whoever the man is that has enchanted Brabantio's daughter, even if it's the Duke's own son, he will get what's coming to him. Brabantio's quick to point out that the man is actually the Duke's current hero, the Moor, Othello.
- The Duke asks Othello what he has to say for himself. Actually, Othello has quite a bit to say: his only offense is to have married Brabantio's daughter. Othello says he's a man of action, so his speech will be a poor defense, but he'll give them the whole story of how he won Brabantio's daughter, and they can then judge whether he's guilty or not.
- Brabantio pipes up and insists that his daughter is as pure as the snow, so there's no way she could come to love the Moor except via his trickery. Othello begs to differ. In fact, he says, they can bring Brabantio's daughter, his new wife, to confirm the story right here and now, if they wish.
- If Othello is in the wrong, the senators may take away his title and order him to be killed. Othello sends Iago, in whom he trusts, to fetch the girl while he tells the story of his courtship.
- Othello explains that Brabantio himself used to invite him over all the time so he (Brabantio) could listen to the fantastic tales of Othello's life, including, but not limited to: daring escapes within a hair's breadth of death; being sold into slavery and getting his

freedom back; and traveling over the world's caves, deserts, quarries, and hills. Also, there were cannibals.

- Whenever Othello would come over, he noticed that Brabantio's daughter, Desdemona, would listen attentively whenever she could. Even when she had to tend to women's work, she'd sneak back to eavesdrop on the stories. Othello convinced Desdemona to ask him to hear his stories, which she clearly wanted to do. (Read that again, it's complicated, but it's important because it implies that their courtship doesn't seem to be one where one person was more actively pursuing the other.)

- Othello then consented to tell her his stories and, upon hearing them, she swooned over Othello's daring. Desdemona then flirted with Othello, saying if he had a friend who could tell his stories (and had his bravery), she'd love that guy.

- Othello takes the hint and says something like, "Well, I tell my stories pretty well, so maybe we should be friends." Othello claims Desdemona loves him for the dangers he had escaped, and he loves her for the pity with which she appreciates his dangerous escapes.

- Just then Iago enters with Desdemona, the lady in question. Brabantio says he'd like to hear from his daughter whether she was willingly part of the courtship. He asks her where she thinks her loyalty should lie. Desdemona says she loves her father, but just like her mother, she must love her husband more than her father.

- Brabantio is not pleased. He says he'll give Desdemona over to Othello, but still, Brabantio is an unhappy man.

- The Duke says Brabantio would only waste his time being sad about what's already over. Besides his bitterness would likely only bring more trouble. Instead, he should just be happy because he doesn't have a choice but to be happy; he doesn't have a say in the affairs of his daughter anymore.

- After Brabantio laments some more, the Duke gets back to the situation in Cyprus. Though they've already got some guys on the ground there, everyone would feel better if Othello went, as he's competent and knowledgeable about the area. The Duke says he's sorry, but Othello will have to spend his wedding night preparing for battle (not knowing he's speaking metaphorically and prophetically).

- Othello says he's happy to go, but insists Desdemona should be taken care of, as with his wedding night interrupted, he hasn't been able to take care of her.

- The Duke suggests that perhaps Desdemona should stay at her father's house, but everyone agrees this is a bad idea.

- Instead, Desdemona suggests she'd like to go with her new husband. She suggests that her love is only complete if she can live with him. Desdemona says she fell in love with Othello's character and profession, and if she's left behind while he's in war, the very qualities she loves will be absent from her.

- The Duke thinks they can settle these domestic disputes on their own. Whether Desdemona is to stay or go, Othello needs to leave for battle NOW. Othello agrees to this, and leaves his trusted friend, Iago, to follow, bringing Desdemona and anything else Othello might need.

- As everyone is parting, the Duke tries to cheer Brabantio, saying Othello is "more fair than black." Brabantio won't have any of it, and warns Othello that he should watch the girl: she's likely to deceive him the way she deceived her own father.

- Othello, in a moment of foreshadowing, responds that his life rests upon Desdemona's faithfulness. Othello instructs Iago to take Desdemona along with Iago's wife, Emilia, on the journey to the battle area.

- After Othello and Desdemona have left, Iago remains with Roderigo. Roderigo announces he will drown himself out of lovesickness (for Desdemona), and Iago chides him for his foolishness. If he's going to be damned for some sin (like suicide), it would be better to be damned for a more practical one, like making money. Iago (who has been spending Roderigo's money like there's no tomorrow) instructs Roderigo to cool his passion with his reason. He then literally tells him nine times that he'd be better off focusing on making money than having true love.
- Iago promises that once Desdemona passions for Othello will eventually cool. Othello will soon surely find he's had enough of Desdemona too, as Moors are known for their changing tastes. Then, Roderigo will have a chance to win Desdemona for himself.
- Iago promises he'll join with the tribes of Hell to make trouble for the marriage of Othello and Desdemona, if Roderigo will only keep making money. Iago reminds Roderigo again that he hates the Moor, and promises to meet Roderigo in the morning, if he hasn't killed himself. Roderigo promises to sell all his land for money instead of killing himself. He then exits.
- Once Roderigo's gone, Iago fills us in on his nasty plan. He's only sporting with Roderigo for fun and profit, but has a bone to pick with Othello, as it's rumored that Othello was sleeping with Iago's wife.
- Iago then figures he'll take Cassio (his competitor) out, too. He hatches a plan to suggest to Othello that Cassio, who has the making of a ladies' man, is having an affair with Desdemona. Iago thinks the Moor is easily influenced, and his suspicion of Cassio will both ruin the great arithmetician's military career and Othello's marriage. Iago declares Hell and night will be his companions in this mischief, and he exits.

Act 2, Scene 1

- You thought there was going to be a battle scene. Instead, it turns out that a really big storm knocked out the entire Turkish fleet, so now Othello will have nothing to do except honeymoon in Cyprus.
- Cassio has arrived before Othello and now converses with the Governor of Cyprus, Montano, about how wonderful Othello and his new wife are. As they await everyone else's arrival, the people onshore in Cyprus are nervous about whether Othello and Desdemona made it through the storm. Cassio hopes they'll both get to Cyprus safely and quickly.
- Desdemona makes it to Cyprus first, along with Iago and his wife, Emilia, who is going to be Desdemona's lady attendant. Cassio welcomes Desdemona and Emilia – flirtatiously kissing Emilia. Iago quips that if Emilia would kiss Cassio's lips as deftly as she whips him (Iago) with her tongue, Cassio would be over her quickly.
- As Iago mocks his wife for being a nag, Desdemona tries to defend her. Desdemona then asks Iago his opinion of women. Iago goes through a series of rhyming racist and sexist jokes. At least we see where Iago stands.
- Iago makes a snide aside to himself, noting how freely Cassio flirts with the women, kissing them and taking their hands to his lips. Iago will gladly make Cassio's hand-kissing his undoing. Iago then says after he's done his part, Cassio will wish his fingers were "clyster

pipes" or enema tubes. (gross!)

- Finally, Othello shows up. He and Desdemona embrace and put on a big show of PDA (public display of affection). Othello says he could die now, as he's so happy to see Desdemona. "God forbid," Desdemona says. They engage in more PDA. After instructing Iago to get his trunks and take the ship's captain to the castle, Othello leaves with Desdemona.
- With everyone else gone, Iago and Roderigo (who have traveled there together) are left to start scheming again. Iago says men in love are known to be more beastly than their natures usually allow, and he plans to take advantage of this.
- Iago tells Roderigo that Desdemona is already over Othello and interested in Cassio. He then gives his longwinded speech, *again*, about how passions tend to cool. As Desdemona got over Othello, Cassio stepped right in, as he's handsome and charming and valiant. Iago offers as proof the fact that Desdemona held Cassio's hand while they greeted each other, which is no evidence at all, unless you're a jealous, murder-plotting lover.
- Conveniently, Cassio will be on the night-watch this evening, so Iago suggests that perhaps Roderigo would like to pick a fight with him, get him demoted, and then have less competition for Desdemona.
- Roderigo agrees. After he exits, Iago gloats to the audience about the success of his scheming. He has actually convinced himself that it's perfectly possible that Desdemona and Cassio might have an affair.
- Iago admits that Othello is a loving husband to Desdemona, but says that he, too, loves Desdemona. Don't forget, the revenge bit seems to stem from Iago thinking Othello had sex with his wife Emilia. He doesn't know for sure, but he's going to assume it's true, as that makes life and crime easier. The thought (of Othello with Emilia) plagues Iago, and he won't be content until he's even, "wife for wife." (This might suggest that Iago wants to defile Desdemona by sleeping with her, or some other means.)
- If he can't explicitly ruin Desdemona, Iago will be contented by making Othello so jealous he can't think straight. If Roderigo does his job right (and picks a fight with Cassio), then Iago can use Cassio as a means to further Othello's jealousy. Iago plans to trash-talk Cassio to Othello, planting suspicion about Cassio's alleged relationship with Desdemona. Iago also clarifies that part of his hatred for Cassio is a suspicion that Cassio, too, has slept with Iago's wife.
- Iago gloats that, despite all this wickedness, Othello will praise him and not realize he is the one orchestrating Othello's madness and downfall. Iago admits his plan isn't perfected yet, but evil never is – until the time comes for it to be done. Mwah-hah-hah.

Act 2, Scene 2

- We're now back on the streets of Cyprus to hear Othello's herald make a public announcement: in celebration of the Turkish fleet's destruction, Othello has declared that tonight will be a party night in Cyprus. Every man can do what pleases him best.

Act 2, Scene 3

- Othello tells Cassio to keep the party under control. Cassio notes that actually that's Iago's job, but sure, he's willing to help out. After Othello says he trusts Iago (bad move), he tells Desdemona he's paid for her by marrying her, and now it's about time that he gets to collect.

- Once Othello leaves, Iago meets with Cassio, all ready to start their night-watch together (they're guarding the court while everyone else gets their party on). Iago notes its actually only 10:00 pm, way too early to start. Obviously, Othello only put them on watch because he had some business to attend to.

- Iago then prods Cassio to talk about how appealing Desdemona is. He tries to get Cassio to call the girl a whore, but Cassio's more of a gentleman than that. When it doesn't work, Iago tries to convince him to drink. He prods Cassio, saying they've got friends coming that would be happy to have a drink in honor of "black Othello." Cassio points out that he's kind of a lightweight, and he's already had his one drink for the night.

- So Iago dismisses Cassio to get the door for the three Cypriot gallants who are now waiting there. Left alone, Iago reveals his master plan of drunkenness: he hopes to get Cassio hammered, knowing that Roderigo's been drinking all night in the name of his lost love. Once the three drunk Cypriots, who are quick to fight when saucy, are tossed in the mix, a rough and tumble night is guaranteed.

- As the young gentlemen of Cyprus (the gallants) enter with Montano and Cassio, Cassio declares they've already given him another drink. Iago, thrilled to bits, sings a drinking song and calls the Danish and Dutch people poor comparisons to a British drunk.

- Iago then sings another song, of a King Stephen who's too distracted by his clothes, and so loses his kingdom. (This is handy if you're reading *The Tempest*, as Shakespeare alludes to this song again when would-be king, Stephano, gets distracted by a wardrobe and so sacrifices his dominion over the island.)

- The point is, everyone's getting sauced. Cassio, lightweight that he is, gets more drunk than everybody else, and begins to moralize about how they shouldn't be drunk, as he'd like his soul to be saved when he dies.

- Iago agrees that he, too, would like his soul saved, but Cassio says Iago should wait to die after him, as lieutenants should have their souls saved before dinky low-ranking flag-boys. Cassio continues undiplomatically that they should all look to their business as though they weren't drunk. He insists that he's not drunk, and he's so not drunk he can even distinguish his right hand from his left hand. Definitely not drunk.

- Cassio then heads off with the other drunken men to start their night watch, leaving Montano, Governor of Cyprus, alone with Iago. Not shockingly, Iago does his usual thing when left alone with someone: he slanders the person that's just left the room.

- Iago says that Cassio's virtues are well balanced with his vices, suggesting the lieutenant is extreme in both his good and bad behavior. Iago adds that Cassio drinks himself to sleep when he can. Montano, hearing this, concludes that Othello is too good-natured to recognize Cassio's alcoholism.

- Roderigo then enters, and Iago sends him off after Cassio. This is a set up for a fight between the two. Iago continues to shoot the breeze with Montano when Roderigo runs in – chased by Cassio. As Cassio hits Roderigo (who literally asked for it), Montano tries to stop him. Naturally, Cassio turns his drunken fury on Montano.

- Iago instructs Roderigo to run and make a ruckus about the fact that a mutiny has started, and then acts all surprised when, shortly after, the town bell is rung (likely by Roderigo). This makes it a sure bet that Othello will come in and ask just what all the fuss is about.
- Then… Othello comes in and asks just what all the fuss is about. Iago feigns innocence and says he doesn't know how the brawl started, he just suddenly saw everyone fighting like they were suddenly transformed to a schoolyard.
- Othello demands explanations: Cassio says he can't speak, and Montano, claiming to be weak from blood-loss, says he's only guilty if he can be blamed for not being able to protect himself.
- So Cassio's drunk, Montano's claiming self-defense, and Othello's mad. He says his passion is beginning to overtake his reason, and everyone's going to get a beating unless this gets cleared up immediately. Further, it's for shame that the men make such a ruckus when the poor people of Cyprus feel like they're at war, and their supposed rescuers can't even manage their own domestic disputes.
- Othello calls on Iago to explain, who claims he would never speak a bad word against Cassio. He says he was chatting with Montano when a fellow ran in crying for help, with Cassio in hot pursuit. Montano, stepping toward Cassio to calm him down, got pulled into the fray.
- Iago continues: he chased after the yelling fellow to stop him from waking the city (mission not accomplished), and Cassio and Montano were embroiled in a fight by the time he came back. (All in all, Iago claims he wants to protect Cassio, but in actuality, deliberately makes Cassio seem to be the one at fault.) Othello thinks Iago's meager report of Cassio's wrong is his attempt to cover for Cassio, which lets him imagine Cassio is even more at fault. Mission accomplished.
- Furious, Othello fires Cassio from his position as one of his officers. Desdemona comes in, confused. Othello tells her to go back to bed, but says in the meantime that he has to take care of the wounded Montano.
- After they leave, Iago pretends to make nice with Cassio, asking if he's OK. Cassio replies that he's mortally wounded, and Iago basically says, unsympathetically, "what a pity." Cassio says in this fight, his reputation has suffered irreparable harm. Iago comforts him, stating that reputation is a stupid marker by which to judge people, as it's earned and lost so easily. Iago claims Cassio has no reputation at all, "unless you repute yourself such a loser."
- Anyway, Iago insists that Cassio can win back Othello's affections, as Othello punished Cassio more because it was immediately necessary than out of any long term hate.
- Iago asks if Cassio remembers why he chased that one guy (Roderigo), and Cassio says he remembers a lot of stuff, but not any particular offense. He goes on to blame wine for a bit, and generally condemns drinking until Iago cuts this off.
- Iago suggests that Cassio go to Desdemona and get her on his side. After all, she and Othello might as well share one mind. Desdemona is so nice, Iago claims, that she'll be eager to help Cassio, and certain to persuade Othello to take him back (as an officer). Cassio thinks this is a grand idea, and says he'll go to Desdemona in the morning.
- Iago is then left alone. As usual, he informs us that he's very pleased with himself. Even if he were an honest guy who was Cassio's friend, he would have given him the same advice: go get help from Desdemona. It just so happens that this "good advice" plays right into Iago's plan to make Othello jealous of Cassio. Gleefully, Iago realizes that Desdemona's own kindness to Cassio will be her own downfall.

- Roderigo comes in, fresh from the beating from Cassio, and says he thinks he should give up and go back to Venice, as now he's poor and bruised up. Iago tells him he has to be patient; though Cassio technically won the fight, the injury against Cassio will have longer effects – the fight's gotten him fired, after all, and who knows what it might bring upon him later.
- Iago dismisses Roderigo and goes back to bad-guy scheming. First, Iago plans to get his wife (Emilia) to try to plead Cassio's case to Desdemona. Second, he will try to get Othello all to himself, and then conveniently lead him to some place where he can chance upon Cassio in intimate private speech with Desdemona, in a classic "it's not what it looks like, honey" moment.

Act 3, Scene 1

- Cassio, eager to please, has sent some musicians to play, badly, in hopes of winning back Othello's good favor. Othello's clown comes out and asks the players why their instruments sound so nasal.
- The clown dismisses the musicians, and Cassio asks him if Desdemona is up yet. Just then, Iago enters and is shocked to see Cassio has not yet gone to bed. (Cassio is eager to make his case to Desdemona.)
- Cassio says he's already sent for Emilia, and Iago promises to send her to Cassio post-haste, so she can hear his plea and make it to Desdemona. In the meantime, Iago promises to lure Othello away from Desdemona, so Cassio can speak with her freely. Iago exits to do more evil master-planning.
- After Cassio praises Iago for his kindness and honesty, Emilia enters and reports that Desdemona is already pleading to Othello on Cassio's behalf. Othello worries that Montano, Cassio's victim, is kind of a big deal in Cyprus, though Othello has decided that his liking for Cassio should be enough to overcome the fact that Cassio has wronged the wrong guy. (There are guys you hit, and there are guys you don't hit. Montano is a guy you don't hit, and Othello is the guy who tells you that.)
- Cassio asks Emilia if perhaps he might speak to Desdemona alone. Emilia goes to see if she can arrange such a meeting.

Act 3, Scene 2

- Cut to Othello and Iago in the citadel. Othello bids Iago to give his regards to the Senate, and instructs him to meet later at the fortifications that are being built. Meanwhile, he's off to inspect said fortifications, which conveniently gets him out of the way for Cassio to have private, incriminating time with Desdemona.

Act 3, Scene 3

- Cassio has explained the whole situation to Desdemona, and she promises to not rest until she's convinced Othello to grant Cassio's acceptance back into the military as well as Othello's personal friendship. Cassio declares he's forever indebted to her, and Desdemona again emphasizes that she'll do everything she can. She even says, "Thy solicitor shall rather die/ Than give thy cause away" (3.3.27-28). Definition: foreshadowing.

- Seeing Othello coming, Cassio decides it's time to leave. Desdemona tells him to stay, but Cassio feels too weird and hurries out. Thus, Iago begins his make-Othello-jealous campaign by commenting on how weird it is that Cassio hurried off so quickly, like a thief stealing away in the night.

- Desdemona jumps right into sweet-talking Othello and campaigning for Cassio. She claims that Cassio is really sorry, and suggests Othello call Cassio back to plead his case. Othello says "not now," and Desdemona says something like, "well, maybe tomorrow, or Tuesday morning, or Tuesday night, or Wednesday morning, or how about Wednesday night?"

- When Othello keeps putting her off, Desdemona claims she would never deny him anything, so why won't he listen to her? Besides, she has his best interests in mind.

- Othello responds that he will deny her nothing, but in the meantime could she please leave him alone.

- Iago asks fake-casual questions about Cassio, whom Othello says was often a go-between when he courted Desdemona. Iago keeps dropping uncomfortable hints, and finally, Othello demands to know what's bothering him. Iago says he'd rather not say, and then Othello presses him, and then Iago says he'd rather not say, and Othello presses.

- Eventually, after Iago has cast doubt on Cassio's honesty, suggested he is disloyal, and hinted that Desdemona is unfaithful, Iago tells Othello, "O beware, my lord, of jealousy; It is the green-eyed monster which doth mock / the meet it feeds on" (3.3.166-168). That's great, except that by "beware" he really means "I hope you become jealous and kill your wife, because that would be ironic."

- Othello says that he's not the type to get jealous – he builds his conclusions upon having suspicions, but only after he investigates them. If something seems wrong, he'll find out what's happening right away and resolve the situation. Othello knows Desdemona is desirable, and that he himself isn't, but that doesn't bother him. "She had eyes and chose me," Othello tells himself (3.3.190).

- Further, Othello promises he has to *see* something to raise his suspicion before he'd have doubts about his wife's loyalty, and if he *were* to see and have doubts, he'd prove whether they were justified right away. This strategy helps him avoid being too influenced in his reason by love or jealousy. It's a good plan, except if it does exist, he doesn't use it.

- Iago essentially says, "OK, if you promise you won't be jealous, you should watch Desdemona with Cassio, but objectively, and not out of jealousy." Iago says he knows well the ways of the women of Venice: they are promiscuous, and though heaven knows their little exploits, their men don't.

- Iago adds helpfully (to help with the objectivity bit) that Desdemona *did* deceive her father in order to marry Othello. He's implying, as Brabantio earlier did, that Desdemona is not to be trusted, as she is a woman, and thus a liar. Basically, Hamlet could get together with these guys and have a big anti-women party. (Frailty, thy name is lying scheming woman!)

- Othello is persuaded by what Iago has said, and it's clear the seed of suspicion has been

planted. Iago tells Othello that he hopes he hasn't ruined his day. This is the trickiest, most dastardly bit of all, because he totally hopes he *has* ruined Othello's day. Who's a liar now?

- Othello assures Iago that he's A-OK, and Iago insists all of his speculations come from a place of love. Further, he tells Othello not to stretch out these suspicions into anything more serious or dangerous.
- Othello promises he isn't much moved, and also, he may still think Desdemona is honest. "Still," Othello falters, "sometimes nature wrongs itself..." Iago seizes on this thought, playing painfully on Othello's insecurity. Iago claims it was against Desdemona's God-given nature to reject all of the suitors who came from her country, had her complexion, and her status.
- Iago contends that Desdemona's unnatural choice against these suitors suggests that other "foul disproportions [and] thoughts unnatural" (3.3.233) might dwell in Desdemona's breast. Iago says he only brings this up to point out that one day, Desdemona might come back to her natural senses, repent her choice to marry Othello, and give him up for someone else less... well... black. (Note that Iago very carefully avoids explicitly saying that marriage to Othello in particular was an unnatural choice, but he exploits the heck out of the *suggestion*.)
- On this despicable note, Iago leaves Othello to brood over the possibility that Desdemona is cheating on him, an undesirable black man. As Othello's busy wondering why he ever got married, Iago comes back to twist the knife a little more.
- Acting regretful, Iago tells Othello not to think about it too much – it's probably nothing, he's probably overreacting, but just in case, Othello should keep an eye out for anything sketchy, especially anything like Desdemona seeming really keen on Cassio getting his position back. Iago once again leaves Othello to his thoughts.
- Now alone, Othello praises Iago for being an honest man, a man insightful about matters of the heart. He then reflects on his relationship with Desdemona, using terminology from the gentleman's sport of falconry: in a rare moment of exquisite vulnerability, Othello compares Desdemona to his falcon. He says if he does find that she is wild (haggard), then, though the leather straps that would tie her to his wrists (jesses) are actually his heart-strings, he would release her to fly on the wind at fortune, both "at random" and "to her fate," though he'd not know if she would ever return to him.
- Othello undercuts this beautifully noble sentiment by thinking of other reasons Desdemona might be unfaithful to him. Whatever it is, Othello concludes Desdemona is lost to him; his only relief from his grief will now be to hate her. (A far cry from the falconry metaphor, we might note!) Othello laments his position: men may say their women belong to them, yet they can never own their women's appetites for love and lust.
- Still, Othello admits he could not bear to let others have even a little of his love's love. He decides this is the inevitable fate of important men: they are destined to be betrayed, even from the moment they're born.
- Emilia and Desdemona come in, and for a moment Othello's mind reverses almost immediately; he can't believe that his wife would betray him. Desdemona has come to bring him to supper, along with the native Cypriots he's invited to dine. But he's not so much ready for the partying; Othello's jealousy has already made him physically ill.
- Desdemona notices her husband seems unwell, and she tries to soothe him, offering to bind up his head with her handkerchief. Othello declares her handkerchief to be too little, and pushes it away from him. The two exit, leaving Emilia alone in the room.

- Emilia's got her eyes on Desdemona's handkerchief, which Othello dropped during his angry moment. Emilia reveals that this was Othello's first love token to his wife, and her husband, Iago, has often asked her to steal it. She hasn't been able to do so yet, as Desdemona loves it like a security blanket. Emilia decides to have the embroidery pattern copied, and then she'll give it to her husband, Iago. (Either handkerchiefs are pretty popular, or women must not have a lot of stuff do, because as you'll soon see, copying patterns of handkerchiefs is all the rage.) She doesn't know what plans he has for it, but like a good wife, she'll make him happy, in the hopes that he'll love her in return.

- Iago comes in and casually mocks his wife, as he usually does. Emilia, proud, produces the handkerchief. She admits she didn't steal it, but that Desdemona let it drop by negligence. If she was expecting praise, she doesn't get it: Iago calls her a "good wench," which maybe passes for a compliment in their relationship. She asks what he intends to do with it before she hands it over, and Iago declares that's none of her business.

- Emilia says that, her business or not, it had better be a good reason, as Desdemona will go mad once she realizes her favorite love token is gone. Iago instructs his wife to forget the whole incident. After he's grabbed the handkerchief, he orders her to leave.

- Iago decides to put the handkerchief (which he also calls a napkin) in Cassio's room, in order to fuel Othello's suspicions. Though the token is only a little thing, it's enough of a confirmation to set off Othello's jealous fantasies about what Cassio might be doing with the handkerchief (and his wife).

- Watching Othello enter again, Iago gloats that none of the drugs in the world could make the man rest easy, now that he's worried about his wife. Othello takes his own turn to curse; he declares it's better to be greatly wronged and know about it than to have just a bit of suspicion that one is wronged.

- Iago acts confused, as though he doesn't understand that Othello is angry at him for planting the seed of suspicion. Othello declares that he would never have suspected Desdemona before, since a man who's robbed of something and doesn't know it is as good as not having been robbed at all. Basically, even if Desdemona is sleeping all over Cyprus, Othello would be better off not knowing about it.

- As it stands, knowing of Desdemona's potential unfaithfulness has destroyed Othello's own identity. His peaceful mind, his happiness, and even his standing as a soldier (especially his joy in the glory of war) are all tainted by this knowledge. Desdemona has unmanned him, and even Othello's proud victories on the battlefield now seem out of reach. He demands that Iago give him proof of Desdemona's cheating on him. If Iago is just playing with him, he's going to really regret it.

- Iago acts all insulted that Othello doesn't trust him, and cries out that it's an awful world where one can be punished so much for their well-intentioned honesty. Othello agrees Iago should be honest, and again demands that he bring him proof of Desdemona's infidelity.

- Iago describes how difficult it would be to prove infidelity; would Othello like to see Desdemona and Cassio caught in the throes of passion? Iago then painstakingly conjures an image of Desdemona and Cassio being passionate together, and says Othello wouldn't like to see that, now would he? The power of the mental image is key here.

- After this vivid description, Othello again presses Iago for some good reason why he should suspect Desdemona. Iago then describes now that at one time he did "lay with Cassio" (as manly bunkmates). Iago was kept up by a toothache, and he was awake to hear, he claims, Cassio mumbling in his sleep.

- Iago recounts: Cassio supposedly called out to Desdemona in his sleep, telling her to be cautious and hide their love. Then, Cassio started writhing around in the bed and kissing Iago's hand as if it were Desdemona. At this point, we're kind of confused as to why Iago wouldn't wake Cassio up and say, "Excuse me, please stop making out with my hand." Anyway, the still-asleep-and-dreaming Cassio then supposedly threw his legs over Iago's thighs, kissed some more, and finally declared, "Cursed fate that gave thee to the Moor!" (3.3.426), in case Iago had left any doubt.
- Othello, not surprisingly, is furious, but Iago is quick to note that this was all just Cassio dreaming, a highly incriminating dream, no doubt, but a dream nonetheless. Regardless, Othello is totally convinced by this story about Cassio in bed.
- Iago, with great timing, puts that final nail in the coffin. Still playing innocent, and instructing Othello to be calm (which only helps his fury), he tells Othello he saw Cassio with Desdemona's special handkerchief.
- Hearing this, Othello announces all his love for Desdemona is gone. He's now out for blood and revenge, hopefully in one convenient package. Iago, hearing this, makes some paltry attempts to remind Othello that they've only got suspicions, but again, this only sharpens Othello's desire for revenge. Othello then kneels and swears that his former love for Desdemona will not stop him from bloodily avenging her betrayal.
- Iago kneels with him and vows to do whatever it takes to help regain honor. Othello asks him to kill Cassio. Iago agrees and slyly adds, "but let her live" (3.3.474), speaking of Desdemona. "Damn her, lewd minx!" Othello curses. Othello's decided that she has to die. To close the scene, Iago declares, "I am your own for ever" (3.3.479), actually meaning that he's totally owned Othello.

Act 3, Scene 4

- Desdemona chats with the clown and asks him to bring a message to Cassio that he should come visit her. She wants the clown to make it clear that she's been good to her word about asking Othello for Cassio's reinstatement. She hopes all will be well.
- The clown exits, and Desdemona is left with Emilia. She asks Emilia where on earth her handkerchief could've gone. Obviously upset to have lost it, Desdemona says that if Othello were the kind of guy to be jealous – which, of course, he isn't – her loss of the handkerchief would make him suspicious. She claims Othello has no such jealousy because the sun of his native land sapped it up from him.
- As Othello approaches the two women, Desdemona declares that she won't leave Othello alone until he's agreed to see Cassio. Othello then enters the scene, clearly failing at his attempt to pretend that nothing's wrong.
- Othello asks Desdemona for her hand, and notes that it is moist, which was thought to be a sure mark of a lascivious person. Othello waxes on about Desdemona's hand; he says it's a hot hand, which means it should turn to prayer and fasting and other chaste pursuits so it doesn't fall victim to the passions.
- He then declares her hand is a frank one, and she interprets it to mean generous (for she says it's the hand that gave away her heart). Othello continues to riff on her perverted sexuality, as "frank" also meant "lusty" or "unable to conceal secrets."

- Othello laments that in the old days, when one gave up their hand in marriage, they gave up their heart. This lengthy interlude is fun with wordplay, but also a scene setting to show Othello is suspicious, but not yet furious at Desdemona, who will walk into her own damnation.
- To make matters worse, Desdemona changes the subject by reminding Othello that he promised to see Cassio (about getting his job back). This, of course, only inflames Othello's suspicions. He declares that his eyes are watering strangely, and asks if perhaps Desdemona has her handkerchief about her. As Desdemona hands him a normal handkerchief, Othello asks her where her *special* handkerchief is. Desdemona simply says she doesn't have it with her, likely because she doesn't want to upset him by saying that it's lost. So instead, she inadvertently upsets him by seeming to confirm that her handkerchief is with her secret lover.
- Othello then tells her the story of the handkerchief. It's a family heirloom and totally sacred. A psychic informed his mom that, as long as she had the handkerchief, Othello's dad would love her. BUT, if she lost it or gave it away, Othello's dad would hate her and go back on the prowl.
- Othello's mom gave the handkerchief to her son on her deathbed, telling him to give it to the woman he'd have for his wife. Othello explains this is why he told Desdemona to take care of the handkerchief, as losing it would be bad. Naturally, this worries Desdemona.
- Othello asks point-blank if the handkerchief is lost. Desdemona hesitates, and then tells something of a lie. "It is not lost," she says (3.4.81). OK, so maybe an outright lie. The discussion over the handkerchief escalates into a huge fight. Othello keeps demanding to see it and Desdemona keeps refusing and telling him that he needs to forgive Cassio (which is really not helping her case about not being Cassio's secret lover). Eventually, Othello storms out, all for the want of a handkerchief.
- Desdemona is shocked. She's never seen this side of her husband, and she doesn't know what's going on. Emilia declares this is no big deal, since women are like food to me.
- Cassio and Iago choose this moment to show up, with Iago encouraging Cassio to make his case to Desdemona. She explains that now is not a great time for them to talk to Othello, since he's in bad spirits, and a little watery-eyed since he's lacking a handkerchief. Iago, all innocence, says that Othello's behavior sounds really strange, but being the good guy that he is, he'll try to find out what's wrong.
- Desdemona slowly convinces herself that she shouldn't be angry at Othello for his behavior. Surely, she reasons, there must be some cause for it beyond the handkerchief, and probably something to do with Othello's work in Venice or Cyprus.
- She decides that sometimes men, worried about big things, take it out on women, over little things.
- Desdemona declares that she is to blame for getting upset at Othello over nothing. Classic enabling. Emilia, who, by the way, is totally at fault, says she hopes that Othello is just upset over things related to work, because it sure seems like he's jealous. "Heaven keep that monster from Othello's mind!" Desdemona prays (3.4.161), which means Shakespeare is repeating metaphors. Desdemona promises Cassio that she'll try again when Othello calms down, and she and Emilia exit, leaving Cassio alone in the scene.
- Then Bianca, a prostitute of sorts and one who is in love with Cassio, comes in and yells at Cassio for not coming to see her often enough. Cassio makes weak excuses – it's clear that he doesn't take her seriously.

- Cassio hands Bianca Desdemona's handkerchief, asking her to copy the pattern. Bianca gets all worried that Cassio has a new woman who's given him this as a token of affection, but Cassio explains that he found the handkerchief in his bedroom (thanks to Iago, unbeknownst to Cassio).
- Cassio thinks surely someone will ask for the lovely handkerchief back, in which case he'd like to have his own copy, so could Bianca please take a break from being a prostitute and do some sewing for him, and also go away as quickly as possible?! After all, the last thing he needs is for Othello to see him with a prostitute.

Act 4, Scene 1

- Enter Iago and Othello. Iago is playing mind games with Othello as usual, forcing him to imagine Desdemona and Cassio in bed together. Iago plays on Othello's lost handkerchief, saying if he'd given it to a woman, it would be her possession, and she'd be free to give it to anyone she pleased. Othello then asks whether her honor could be given as freely, too. He had forgotten about the handkerchief until Iago graciously reminded him.
- Iago wheedles a bit more, now making the outright lie that Cassio claims to have lain with Desdemona. Othello gets so upset he starts mumbling and falls into a trance.
- As Iago gloats over the effects of his wicked work, Cassio comes in and wonders what's going on with Othello. Iago explains that he's just having a fit – totally normal – in fact, the second one since yesterday. Cassio suggests that perhaps they should try to tend to Othello, but Iago thinks it best to let the man suffer. He tells Cassio to hang out for a minute and come back when Othello has left, so they can have a friendly chat.
- Othello slowly comes out of his fit. Iago asks if his head still hurts, and Othello, still in a passion, interprets this to mean Iago is thinking any man's head would hurt, if it were burdened by cuckold's horns. (Cuckolds are men who are led about by the horns by their wives. Othello, tricked by his own woman, feels he wears such horns.) Iago "comforts" Othello by saying lots of men are deceived by their women, it's like a club of whipped brothers. Othello then declares Iago to be very wise. All is lost.
- Iago tells Othello to hide a little ways away so that he can overhear a conversation between Iago and Cassio, one where Cassio will clearly incriminate himself by talking loosely about Desdemona. Othello thinks this is a wonderful idea, and says he'll listen with patient and bloody thoughts. (Apparently, finding objective proof has gone out the window.)
- Iago then announces his plan (to us, not Othello): he'll talk in veiled terms to Cassio about Bianca (the prostitute), whom Cassio takes very lightly. Othello, hearing the conversation, is bound to think Cassio is making light of his wife, Desdemona. Iago underhandedly will have given Othello the shadow of proof. Mwah-hah-hah, yet again.
- When Cassio comes back, Iago brings up Bianca, in all her pathetic ardor. Cassio, of course, laughs about how much the woman loves him, how desperate she is, and how easily beguiled she has been by his false intentions of marriage. (This conversation is overheard by Othello, who apparently missed the key word "Bianca." Othello indeed thinks they are talking about his wife.)
- It must be Iago's lucky day, because Bianca herself comes in and throws Desdemona's

handkerchief in Cassio's face. Cassio calls her a "fitchew," which is a polecat, known for being lusty and smelly.

- Bianca is furious that Cassio has given her something that obviously came from another woman, a woman who is indeed a "hobby-horse" (another useful slang term for an Elizabethan harlot). Bianca walks out in a huff and Cassio follows her.

- Othello is completely convinced by this little scene, and furious that Desdemona would give Cassio their special handkerchief, especially since his mother's dying bequest ended up in the hands of a common prostitute. He rages for a bit, and finally gets to talk of action.

- Othello first threatens to chop Desdemona up into little bits. Then, he asks Iago to get him some poison, so he might kill her that very night. He won't chat with her about her offenses, as he's sure she'd be able to talk him out of her murder.

- Othello thinks this murder plan is most just. Iago reveals he still intends to take out Cassio. He assures Othello he'll report back before midnight.

- The conversation is interrupted by Lodovico, kinsman of Brabantio (Desdemona's father, remember?). Lodovico brings news from the Duke in Venice: Othello has been called back to the city, and Cassio is to replace him as command in Cyprus. While Othello reads the letter from the Duke, Lodovico talks with Desdemona (who showed up in the meantime) and asks her how Cassio is doing.

- Desdemona explains how Cassio and Othello had a falling out, and declares she hopes they can work it out "for the love I bear to Cassio" (4.1.233), which is not a good move given the fact that Othello was just thinking about Cassio having sex with his wife. Othello, overhearing Desdemona's loving comments toward Cassio, gets enraged and hits Desdemona.

- Desdemona can't figure out why her husband would strike her – and in public – when she's done nothing to deserve it. Lodovico insists Othello make amends with the poor girl, as she's weeping. Othello insists she can cry crocodile tears (full of falsehood) and he won't care, as she changes faces so easily.

- Othello then declares he'll head back to Venice, and Cassio shall have his post (leaving out that he will be too dead to fill it). Desdemona leaves, shell-shocked, and Othello stalks out muttering, "goats and monkeys!" (4.1.256).

- Lodovico is shocked that Othello would injure his wife and behave so boorishly in public. He wonders whether Othello has been put into a passion by the Duke's letters, but Iago suggests this poor form is Othello's status quo. Iago demurs on giving details about Othello's failings, saying, with seeming humility, that it's not up to him to reveal the evils he's seen. This leaves Lodovico free to imagine worse evils.

Act 4, Scene 2

- We open with Othello grilling Emilia, trying to get her to confess that Desdemona and Cassio are having an affair. Emilia tells him that he's crazy – she has observed Cassio and Desdemona every minute they were together, and nothing remotely suspicious happened. She is sure that Desdemona is honest, if ever there were an honest woman. Emilia insists that only some wretch could have put this thought into his head.

- Othello then sends Emilia to get Desdemona, dismissing her claims as the simple

testimony of a simple woman. Othello has convinced himself that Desdemona is cunning in her harlotry, and it's no surprise she wouldn't be found out, even by her woman friend.

- Apprehensively, Desdemona enters. Othello flies into a passion, falling into tears. Othello accuses Desdemona of being false (particularly, by cheating on him), but Desdemona denies it and tries to argue otherwise.

- She then suggests Othello's rage might be inspired by the letter he received earlier today calling him back to Venice. Desdemona wonders if perhaps Othello thinks the summons to leave Cyprus (and her) were the machinations of her angry father back in Venice. Still, she says if her father had a hand in this, she's not to blame, as she remains staunchly on Othello's side.

- Still, Othello mourns his mystery loss; he says he could bear any amount of suffering from the world, and proceeds to detail any and all types, including sores, poverty, slavery, and a world of scorn. With any of these, he says, he could have patience – but he cannot bear this abuse of his heart.

- Desdemona begs him to tell her what she has done wrong, and Othello calls her a whore and a strumpet. Desdemona swears on her soul that she has never touched anybody but him, but he doesn't believe her.

- Emilia walks in on this little exchange, so Othello takes to abusing her, too. He praises her for being the gatekeeper to Hell, and tells her that she'd do best to keep the events of this night to herself. Othello then exits, and we're all left with raised eyebrows.

- Emilia questions Desdemona worriedly about Othello's behavior, wondering what's happened to her "lord." She then declares that she *has* no lord, nor does she have tears to cry, and no answer is appropriate about what is going on with Othello except an answer that could be told in tears.

- Desdemona bids Emilia to lay her (Desdemona's) wedding sheets on the quarreling lovers' bed tonight, and asks to have Iago come and talk to her. Alone, she resents bearing all this abuse, mostly because she's done nothing wrong.

- Emilia returns with Iago, and Desdemona says she can't even begin to convey what Othello called her. Thankfully, Emilia can! She then lists off that Othello called Desdemona a whore and all sorts of other cruel names. She also reminds Desdemona that she turned down all sorts of nice, rich Venetian boys, even her father, and her friends, and her country… all to marry Othello.

- She also suggests that it could only be some really vile person, seeking his own self interest, that plied Othello with lies about Desdemona's faithfulness in order to make him jealous. She prattles on about this for a while, and Iago tells her to speak quietly, but Emilia notes that it was a very similar scheme, lies from a lying liar, that made Iago believe Othello had been with her too. Iago tells Emilia to shut up already.

- Desdemona begs Iago to tell her what to do, or go talk to Othello on her behalf, to cure him of his wrong-mindedness. She can't believe this is happening to her – as she truly loves Othello. She can't even imagine going behind his back to be with somebody else.

- Iago tells Desdemona not to worry – Othello is probably just upset about state business. He points out that the messengers from Venice are waiting to eat with the women, which is clearly more important than Othello's inexplicable and murderous rage. Iago promises "things shall be well" (4.2.171), and Desdemona and Emilia leave Iago alone.

- Roderigo comes in to yell at Iago for not yet setting him up with Desdemona but still spending all of his (Roderigo's) money. Roderigo's finally starting to wise up to the fact that Iago is just using him for his cash, and in fact never really cared about him.

- Roderigo, who seems rather broke at the moment, wants to know what happened to all the expensive jewelry he gave Iago to give to Desdemona. Iago kept promising that Desdemona was getting the gifts and wanted to give something up in return, but he has yet to see any special favors of Othello's wife.
- Roderigo then throws down the gauntlet – he declares that he'll go and see Desdemona himself. If she returns his jewels, he'll repent ever having tried to court a married woman. But if she has no jewels to return, then Roderigo will take it out on Iago.
- Iago, hearing Roderigo threaten him, declares him a much better man than he'd ever taken him for. Iago insists he's actually been working on the situation and that Roderigo will be all up in Desdemona's jewels come tomorrow night. All Roderigo has to do is listen to Iago's plan.
- Iago informs Roderigo that Othello's been called back to Venice, and Cassio is to replace him in Cyprus. Iago also casts random lies, claiming Othello is headed to Mauritania (in Africa) with Desdemona. If Roderigo were to get rid of Cassio, then Othello couldn't leave Cyprus. (Presumably, this would give Roderigo access to Desdemona.)
- Anyway, Iago quite expertly calms Roderigo down and convinces him that he needs to kill Cassio that very night, probably while Cassio is having dinner with his harlot (Bianca) who, it seems, forgave him for the whole handkerchief thing. Iago promises he'll be right behind him to help with the murdering. Iago declares all of this should go down sometime between midnight and one in the morning. Iago is clear: murdering Cassio is the only way to get to Desdemona. Roderigo, ever a wit, points out that this plan really doesn't make any sense. Somehow Roderigo is appeased when Iago promises he'll explain it all later.

Act 4, Scene 3

- After dinner, Othello suggests a walk with Lodovico and orders Desdemona to get ready for bed. He promises to meet her there soon, and demands that she send Emilia away. The men exit, leaving the women to chat and get ready for bed.
- Emilia notes that Othello looked to be in better spirits, but she's shocked that he told Desdemona to get rid of her. Desdemona just shrugs it off – she can't risk upsetting Othello now. Emilia says she wishes Desdemona had never seen the man. But Desdemona responds that she loves Othello, so much that she would rather be with him, even when he's being totally strange, than live without him.
- Desdemona is in a strange mood that foreshadows her coming death. She randomly tells Emilia that if she should die before her maid, she wishes to be buried wrapped in her wedding sheets. She then sings a song she learned from a maid of her mother's, who had been forsaken by her lover. She admits it was an old song, but it did well to bear out the maid's fate, as she died singing it.
- Emilia tries to change the subject by noting how handsome Lodovico is, but Desdemona is stuck fast to this weird, mourning mood. She begins to sing the song about the willow, which is bad news, as willows are symbolic of disappointed love. (Remember in *Hamlet*, Shakespeare killed Ophelia off by having her "fall" out of a willow tree, mad with the double disappointed loves of her dead father and scornful Hamlet.)
- So this song is essentially about a woman who excuses her awful lover because she loves

him so much. The woman in the song doesn't blame him at all, but when she calls him a cheating jerk, he declares that the more women he gets with, the more likely she is to seek out other men. Desdemona sadly laments, "these men, these men!" (4.3.60).

- She and Emilia then converse about whether women are ever as awful to their men as men are to their women. Emilia is certain this is the case, especially when it comes to cheating. Desdemona asks whether Emilia would ever cheat on Iago, and Emilia, much older and more cynical, tells her that plenty of women cheat. She says you could justify cheating in lots of different ways.

- Desdemona declares she couldn't imagine ever doing such a thing, which leads Emilia to a bit of a rant. Emilia argues that women have the same need for sexual affairs. Since men change their women sportingly, women should have the same option.

- She continues. Some men deserve to be cheated on; it's the husband's fault, not the wife's, if a woman has an affair. After all, she'd only be following the lead of her faithless husband. Desdemona bids Emilia farewell after listening to this sad speech from a sad woman whose husband obviously hates her and is now vindictively sleeping with other women. Desdemona hopes she can use others' bad behavior as a guide of what *not* to do, instead of an excuse to behave badly.

Act 5, Scene 1

- Iago and Roderigo wait in a darkened street for Cassio to come. Iago has given Roderigo a sword. He tries to slip off in the darkness, so as to NOT help with the murder, and Roderigo asks him to stay near, in case he needs any help killing Cassio. Despite the plea, Iago gets away, and Roderigo is left mostly alone and noting to himself that he doesn't really have any ill will towards Cassio. Still, Iago's made a convincing enough argument that the man must die.

- Iago explains his devious plot (again, to us, not to Roderigo) in the cover of the shadows: If Roderigo lives, he'll demand all the jewels and gifts he gave to Iago, intended for Desdemona. (Of course, these were never delivered.) If Cassio lives, his goodness will only remind everyone that, by contrast, Iago is really evil. Also, Cassio is the only one (besides Desdemona) who has the power to clear up what's really going on to Othello. In short, Iago will be glad if either or both men die (meaning Roderigo and/or Cassio).

- Cassio then enters the street and Roderigo, hidden by darkness, tries to stab him. Cassio avoids the thrust, and wounds him back in self-defense. But then Iago arrives unseen and stabs Cassio in the leg.

- Cassio cries out for help from whatever dark alley they all happen to be in. Othello, apparently nearby in his own dark alley, hears the pitiful pleas. Thinking Iago has done away, as he promised, with Cassio, Othello is now full of the piss and vinegar required to go and murder his innocent, faithful beloved. But first, he makes a rousing speech about lust and blood and all that grave stuff. *Then* he exits, presumably to kill Desdemona.

- Lodovico and Gratiano, two Venetian gentlemen, come in when they hear Cassio screaming in the dark. Afraid this may be a trap, they hesitate, leaving Iago some time to enter with a light, the picture of confused innocence. Iago makes a big show of recognizing Cassio as a lieutenant and then vows to seek around in the dark for Cassio's assailant. Of

course, Iago discovers Roderigo, and pretends not to know who he is. Then he conveniently and mortally stabs him.

- Lodovico and Gratiano finally have their wits about them when Bianca enters, in hysterics to find her Cassio wounded in the leg. Iago tries to blame the whole messy situation on the poor strumpet, and then pretends to discover the man no one saw him stab.

- Iago feigns surprise at the fact that Cassio's assailant was none other than Roderigo, who he declares to be his great friend. As they all tend to the wounded Cassio, Iago asks Cassio if there was some beef with Roderigo. Cassio says he doesn't even know the guy, and Iago quickly has the two Venetian gentlemen turn their eyes towards Bianca, who Iago suggests is somehow involved in this whole sordid matter.

- Emilia comes in, and Iago sums up a version of the story through his lying teeth: Roderigo, who is now dead, joined with some other fellows, who are now escaped, to assault Cassio, who is now wounded. Iago, who is now telling the story, is still lying, so everything's fairly status quo.

- Iago then instructs Emilia to inform Othello and Desdemona of all of these very surprising events. Left alone, Iago comments that this night will make him or break him. As it's already broken Roderigo, Cassio, Othello, and Desdemona, take a guess where the odds are stacked.

Act 5, Scene 2

- Othello is a veritable wreck. He entreats the stars to look on his deed as punishing a crime, not as though he's committing a crime himself – it's important to him to declare that he is not the criminal of this whole sordid affair. He promises he'll not mar Desdemona's beautiful skin by cutting her up or anything – she'll be pretty in death.

- Othello now notes the single candle he's brought into the bedroom, where he's found Desdemona sleeping. "Put out the light, and then put out the light," he says (5.2.10), looking at Desdemona. Othello muses that if he puts out the candle, he can easily light it again, but once he kills Desdemona, there is no way of getting her back.

- Othello, during his moment, is almost overwhelmed by his love for Desdemona as he bends to kiss her. He says her beauty is almost enough to stop him from being an agent of justice. Notice how we said "almost" twice? Well, so did Othello, because feelings aside, he promises to kill her and love her after. He weeps over her, lamenting that he must kill what he loves most, alluding to the Biblical passage, Hebrews 12:6: "For whom the Lord loveth he chasteneth."

- All this weeping and kissing and murderous plotting wakes Desdemona. Sleepily, she asks Othello if he's coming to bed. He asks her if she has prayed. "I would not kill thy soul," he says (5.2.32). (Think *Hamlet* again, like when Claudius almost dies.) Desdemona freaks out about the killing bit, and Othello doesn't deny, yes, I intend to kill you. He again asks her to think on her sins, so she can be absolved before she dies (and so go to Heaven instead of Hell).

- Othello then brings up the handkerchief (which we've dubbed the handkerchief of death). He accuses Desdemona of giving it (among other things) to Cassio, and she tries to be very calm in convincing Othello that he has made a mistake. She denies ever having loved

Cassio. Othello says that she's lying and that Cassio is already dead. Desdemona mourns Cassio, whom she says has been betrayed.

- Still, she won't stop fighting for her life. Rather than come out with the story of having simply lost the handkerchief and try to clear up the whole matter, she begs to be banished rather than killed – to be killed tomorrow – to be given just half an hour more to live. But Othello is relentless, and smothers her with a pillow.
- Emilia knocks at the door and calls out for Othello. Desdemona is still not quite dead, so Othello smothers her a little more. He gets lost in his thoughts about how he has no wife.
- Finally inside, Emilia reports (wrongly) that Roderigo has been killed by Cassio, and that Cassio is wounded, but not dead. Othello is furious to realize that Cassio is still alive. But so is Desdemona – for at least three more seconds. "O falsely, falsely murdered!" she says weakly (5.2.117). Desdemona declares she is guiltless, but when Emilia asks her who murdered her, she refuses to name Othello. "Nobody. I myself," Desdemona says. Desdemona finally dies asking Emilia to give Othello her love (5.2.124).
- Othello admits he killed Desdemona and tells Emilia she deserved it, and that honest Iago, Emilia's own husband, can tell her all about it. "My husband?" (5.2.144) Emilia keeps repeating, as the truth slowly dawns on her and she knows she married a jerk. Othello tries to get Emilia to calm down, mostly through his threatening looks, but she says she doesn't care about any harm he can do her. She continues to shout about the murder.
- Soldiers and citizens of Cyprus crowd into the room, along with Iago. Emilia confronts her husband and asks if he told Othello that Desdemona was cheating on him. Iago admits that he suggested this, but then claims that Othello's own suspicion filled in all the blanks.
- Emilia continues to lament Desdemona, and Othello continues to insist that Desdemona was false to him. Gratiano then announces that it's a good thing Desdemona's dad, Brabantio, died of heartbreak over her wedding to Othello, because he really wouldn't have survived traumatic event.
- Othello continues to lay blame on Desdemona's foulness, and Iago keeps trying to silence the lamenting Emilia. Finally, the whole story clears up when Othello says that he saw Desdemona's handkerchief in Cassio's hand, and Emilia tells him that she herself stole the handkerchief and gave it to Iago.
- With this small fact, Iago's whole story begins to unravel. Othello, furious, tries to stab Iago, but Iago avoids him, and instead stabs his wife to death (seemingly), and runs out. Montano bids someone to follow the villain, but only Othello and the slow, dramatically dying Emilia are left. Emilia wonders aloud about the meaning of Desdemona's final song, and she herself dies singing about willows, charging "the Moor" with some serious cruelty. Emilia dies next to Desdemona and tells Othello with her last breath that his wife was pure and faithful to him.
- Othello finally realizes what he has done and curses himself. He finds a sword of Spain he keeps in the bedroom, and thinks suicidal thoughts.
- Othello declares he's seen much worse in battle than this, but no man can escape his fate. He announces that no one has any reason to fear on seeing his weapon, as he's reached his journey's end. He then looks on his wife, murdered by his own hand, though innocent, he's now realized, and Othello weeps to end all days.
- Lodovico, the wounded Cassio, and Montano enter with a recently captured Iago. Othello pronounces Iago to be a devil, and wounds him. Iago lets us know that he's not dead yet. Othello responds that he wouldn't wish such a peaceful fate as death on Iago (as Othello is preparing to meet such a fate). As Lodovico points out that grieving doesn't get you out

of a murder charge, Othello says he can be called a murderer, but it's important to note that he did everything in honor, not in hate.

- Othello demands that Iago tell him why he chose to torment him and ruin his life. "Demand me nothing. What you know, you know," Iago says. "From this time forth, I will never speak word" (5.2.303-304). Lodovico then brings out the papers that will clear the entire mess up. Roderigo, conveniently, had a bunch of mixed letters on his person that explain, in detail, Iago's complicity in all of these plots.

- Othello, finally faced with Cassio, Othello learns that Desdemona was innocent and that everything that happened was part of Iago's scheme. And Roderigo lived long enough to reveal that his murderer was actually... Iago.

- Lodovico orders that Othello be brought back to Venice for his punishment, and announces Cassio is to replace him. Othello wishes to say a word before he goes. He asks that he not be spoken of untruthfully, or in malice, as this tragedy is committed to history.

- Othello declares himself the "one who loved not wisely, but too well," and then sums up the bulk of the play. In his final note, Othello pulls out a hidden weapon and stabs himself, declaring himself a circumcised dog. He has done an evil thing, but by killing himself, had conquered the villain (himself) and therefore become the hero of his own story. Othello kisses Desdemona's dead lips and then dies himself, a murderer, martyr, and lover to the end.

- Lodovico tells Iago to look at his work: three innocent people lying next to each other, all destroyed by his scheming. Still, Iago keeps his promise and stays silent. Gratiano is to inherit all of Othello's worldly goods, and Montano is charged with punishing the wicked Iago. Sadly, Lodovico decides that all he can do is go back to Venice to share this tragic tale.

Themes

Theme of Jealousy

Othello is the most famous literary work that focuses on the dangers of jealousy. The play is a study of how jealousy can be fueled by mere circumstantial evidence and can destroy lives. (In *Othello*, the hero succumbs to jealousy when Iago convinces him that Desdemona has been an unfaithful wife – in the end, Othello murders his wife and then kills himself.) It is interesting that Iago uses jealousy against Othello, yet jealousy is likely the source of Iago's hatred in the first place. In *Othello*, jealousy takes many forms, from sexual suspicion to professional competition, but it is, in all cases, destructive.

Questions About Jealousy

1. What language does Shakespeare use to describe jealousy in the play? Do different characters use different metaphors to describe jealousy, or are there common ways of talking about it?
2. Do other characters besides Othello demonstrate jealousy? In what ways?
3. Is jealousy portrayed as intrinsically unreasonable? Is there a kind of jealousy that is

reasonable, or does the play suggest that all jealousy tends to "mock" the person who is jealous?

4. Why is sexual jealousy the focus of the play, rather than a different kind of jealousy? What other kinds of jealousy are included in Othello? (If you're thinking of Iago's jealousy of Othello, keep in mind that this, too, could be sexual jealousy.)

Chew on Jealousy

The reason Iago chooses to hurt Othello by making him jealous is that Iago is consumed by jealousy himself.

In *Othello,* Shakespeare proves that jealousy is inherently unreasonable, as it is founded on the psychological issues of the jealous person, not on the behavior of the one who prompts the jealous feelings.

Theme of Race

Othello is one of the first black heroes in English literature. A military general, he has risen to a position of power and influence. At the same time, however, his status as a black-skinned foreigner in Venice marks him as an outside and exposes him to some pretty overt racism, especially by his wife's father, who believes his daughter's interracial marriage can only be the result of Othello's trickery. Because the play portrays fears of miscegenation (the intermixing of races via marriage and/or sex), it's nearly impossible to talk about race in *Othello* without also discussing gender and sexuality.

Questions About Race

1. Which characters in the play make an issue of Othello's race? What kinds of stereotypes are at work in this play?
2. How does Othello's race affect his relationships to his wife and to other characters?
3. How does Othello's race play a role in the hero's self-identity?

Chew on Race

In *Othello,* Shakespeare creates a hero who is not a racist stereotype. Despite this, Shakespeare ultimately allows Othello to succumb to the subtle racism that surrounds him.

Othello views his own racial identity as undesirable, and it is this lack of confidence in himself that allows Iago to persuade him that Desdemona is cheating on him.

Theme of Gender

Gender relations are pretty antagonistic in *Othello*. Unmarried women are regarded as their fathers' property and the play's two marriages are marked by male jealousy and cruelty (both wives are murdered by their own husbands). Most male characters in *Othello* assume that *all*

Venetian women are inherently promiscuous, which explains why female sexuality is a *huge* threat to men in the play. Othello is easily convinced his wife is cheating on him and feels emasculated and humiliated as a result.

We should also note that it's impossible to discuss gender and sexuality without considering race – several characters in the play, including Othello, believe that black men sexually contaminate white women, which may partially explain why Othello sees his wife as soiled. See also our discussions of "Race" and "Sex" for more on this topic.

Questions About Gender

1. What kinds of assumptions do male characters make about women? How do male characters view female sexuality in the play?
2. Do male characters ever feel emasculated? If so, when? What triggers such feelings?
3. When Iago tells Brabantio that Othello has eloped with his daughter, why does he call Othello a "thief"? What kinds of assumptions about daughters are being made here?
4. Why does Desdemona want to go to war with Othello?

Chew on Gender

In the play, most male characters assume that women are naturally promiscuous, even if there's no concrete evidence to support such ideas.

Othello is like Shakespeare's *The Merchant of Venice* in that both plays feature fathers who view their unmarried daughters as their property.

Theme of Sex

Shakespeare's play explores some common sixteenth century anxieties about miscegenation (interracial sex and marriage) by examining the relationship between a black man who marries a white woman, accuses her of being unfaithful, and then strangles her on her wedding sheets. In *Othello*, most male characters assume that women are inherently promiscuous, which explains why all three women characters in the play are accused of sexual infidelity. It also explains, in part, why it's possible for Iago to so easily manipulate Othello into believing his wife is having an affair. *Othello* is also notable for its portrayal of homoerotic desire, which seems to be a factor in Iago's plot to destroy Othello and Desdemona.

Questions About Sex

1. Why does Brabantio object to Desdemona's marriage to Othello?
2. How does Iago describe Othello's sexual relationship with Desdemona? How does Iago's attitude about race factor into his description of Othello and Desdemona's lovemaking?
3. Is there any textual evidence of homoerotic desire in *Othello*?
4. What is the role of Bianca, a Venetian courtesan and one of the play's three female characters?

Chew on Sex

In the course of the play, Iago infects Othello with his negative, crude view of sexuality.

To the men in *Othello*, female sexuality is a threatening force more than it is an attractive one.

Theme of Marriage

Shakespeare's portrayal of marriage is pretty bleak in *Othello*. The play begins with a conflict between Desdemona's husband and her father, who sees his daughter's elopement as a kind of theft of his personal property. The play's two wives (Desdemona and Emilia) are both unfairly accused of infidelity, and both wives are murdered by their abusive husbands. More famously, perhaps, is the way Shakespeare examines sixteenth-century anxieties about interracial couplings – in *Othello*, the marriage of a black man and a white woman allows Shakespeare to explore attitudes about race and gender.

Questions About Marriage

1. How are marriages portrayed in *Othello*? Are there any happy marriages in the play? Why or why not?
2. Why does Iago say Othello may have had an affair with Emilia?
3. Why does Othello suspect Desdemona of being unfaithful? Does he have any concrete evidence to support his suspicions?
4. Discuss why Brabantio objects to Desdemona's elopement with Othello.

Chew on Marriage

In *Othello*, marriage is tantamount to death.

Othello suggests that, as long as men view women as being promiscuous and disloyal, the institution of marriage is doomed.

Theme of Manipulation

Othello's villain, Iago, may be literature's most impressive master of deception. Iago plots with consummate sophistication, carefully manipulating Othello (without any real proof) into believing that Desdemona has been unfaithful. His understanding of the human psyche is phenomenal, as is his ability to orchestrate a complicated interweaving of pre-planned scenarios. Iago's deception is potent because of his patience, his cleverness, and what seems to be his intrinsic love of elegant manipulation.

Questions About Manipulation

1. Why does Iago want to manipulate Othello into believing Desdemona has been unfaithful?
2. How is it that Iago is so successful at manipulating everyone around him?

3. How does Iago's openness with the audience contrast with his treatment of other characters? Are WE ever manipulated by Iago's lies?
4. Is Iago's masterful manipulation of the characters in Othello plausible? Why or why not?

Chew on Manipulation

In *Othello*, Iago orchestrates Othello's downfall like a skillful playwright.

Iago's ultimate deception is not of Othello, Cassio, or Roderigo: it is of the audience. By refusing to tell Othello his motivations in Act 5, he is also refusing to tell us. We are strung along through *Othello* in the belief that all will be revealed, but it seems that the joke is on us.

Theme of Warfare

Since the play's protagonist is a military general, war is always hovering in the background in *Othello*. But the only actual battle the play promises is avoided, thanks to bad weather. The real battleground of the play, it turns out, is the mind. Many critics read *Othello* as an extended war allegory; it is possible to see Iago's machinations as the strategic planning of a general, individual victories as minor battles, and the three resulting deaths the casualties of psychological combat. The play also dwells on the relationship between masculine identity, war, and sexuality.

Questions About Warfare

1. How does Othello's profession as a general shape his sense of identity?
2. Does Othello seem torn between his role as a soldier and his role as a lover? If so, when? Why can't he be both?
3. Why does Desdemona want to join Othello in Cypress?
4. Do characters ever use the language of warfare to describe their domestic disputes?

Chew on Warfare

Othello is uncomfortable with being a lover, and this makes it easier for Iago to sway him from being gentle and loving to being a furious killer.

Theme of Hate

Hatred is supposed to have a cause, some concrete event or insult that inspires a lasting rage. But in *Othello*, the play's villain is motivated by a hatred that seems to elude any reasonable definition. Iago's hatred and his determination to destroy his boss, Othello, seems out of proportion with the reasons he gives for it: anger that Othello did not promote him or jealousy that Othello might have slept with Iago's wife. Iago's loathing has been famously called a "motiveless malignancy" that redefines our understanding of hatred, making it seem a self-propelling passion rather than the consequence of any particular action.

Questions About Hate

1. When in *Othello* is the word "hate" used explicitly? What other words are sometimes substituted for "hate"?
2. How does Iago describe his hatred? How often does Iago use the word "love" in comparison with other characters? What kind of relationship might this depict between love and hate? Are they polar opposites, or two shades of the same color?
3. We argued elsewhere in this module that Cyprus, being the "island of Venus," inflames passion in the characters. Does it inflame hatred the same way it does love?

Chew on Hate

In *Othello*, love and hate are shown to be two sides of the same emotion.

Iago is a force that converts everything into its opposite – above all, love becomes hate.

Just as Iago transforms Othello's love into hatred, the play subtly suggests that Iago's hatred for Othello is actually suppressed love.

Theme of Identity

In *Othello*, Shakespeare explores factors that play an important role in the formations of one's identity – race, gender, social status, family relationships, military service, etc. *Othello* is also concerned with how an individual's sense of identity (which can break down and be manipulated by others) shapes his or her actions.

Questions About Identity

1. Does Othello's identity transform over the course of the play? What about Desdemona's?
2. How does Othello and Desdemona's relationship impact each of the characters' identities?
3. Why does Cassio lament that he's lost his "reputation"?
4. Do we ever get a chance to see the real Iago? Why or why not?

Chew on Identity

Othello's rage at Desdemona's infidelity has nothing to do with his love for her; rather, for him, it signals the destruction of his own identity as a successful and loved man.

In *Othello*, a man's reputation seems to hinge on military duty and public behavior, while a woman's identity often hinges on her sexual reputation.

Iago's true identity is ultimately unknowable – for the play's characters as well as the audience.

Quotes

Jealousy Quotes

IAGO
One Michael Cassio, a Florentine,
A fellow almost damn'd in a fair wife;
That never set a squadron in the field,
Nor the division of a battle knows
More than a spinster; unless the bookish theoric,
Wherein the toged consuls can propose
As masterly as he: mere prattle, without practise,
Is all his soldiership. But he, sir, had the election:
And I, of whom his eyes had seen the proof
At Rhodes, at Cyprus and on other grounds
Christian and heathen, must be be-lee'd and calm'd
By debitor and creditor: this counter-caster,
He, in good time, must his lieutenant be (1.1.2)

Thought: Here, Iago claims he hates Othello because Othello passed him, Iago, over for a promotion, giving "one Michael Cassio" the job as his military lieutenant instead. Iago claims he's far more qualified than Cassio, who lacks Iago's experience on the field of battle. Clearly, Iago seems pretty jealous. But is this the *real* reason Iago sets out to destroy Othello? Or, is this merely an excuse to go after him? In other words, does Iago say all of this in order to manipulate Roderigo? (Roderigo, as we soon learn, is completely envious of Othello for marrying Desdemona.)

IAGO
I hate the Moor:
And it is thought abroad, that 'twixt my sheets
He has done my office: I know not if't be true;
But I, for mere suspicion in that kind,
Will do as if for surety. (1.3.12)

Thought: Now this is interesting. Earlier, Iago said he hates Othello because "the Moor" passed him over for a promotion. Yet, here, Iago says he hates Othello because he's heard a rumor that Othello has been hooking up with Iago's wife, Emilia, "twixt [Iago's] sheets." Iago says he doesn't exactly know if the rumor's true, but he's decided to go ahead and ruin Othello's life anyway. Seems like Iago has listed a couple of incompatible motives for seeking to destroy Othello, wouldn't you say? So, we're just not sure we can believe that Iago's jealous of Othello's supposed relationship with Emilia.

Cassio's a proper man: let me see now:
To get his place and to plume up my will
In double knavery--How, how? Let's see:--
After some time, to abuse Othello's ear
That he is too familiar with his wife.
He hath a person and a smooth dispose
To be suspected, framed to make women false.
The Moor is of a free and open nature,
That thinks men honest that but seem to be so,
And will as tenderly be led by the nose
As asses are.
I have't. It is engender'd. Hell and night
Must bring this monstrous birth to the world's light. (1.3.12)

Thought: A few lines earlier (see above passage), Iago claimed that he suspects Othello has been sleeping with his wife, Emilia. Here, Iago shares his plot to destroy Othello with the audience – since Othello is so gullible, Iago will lead him "by the nose," making Othello believe that his, Othello's, wife is having an affair with Cassio. Iago plans to plant the seeds of jealousy in Othello. What's interesting about this passage is the way Iago sees his evil plan as a "monstrous birth," a thing that he will bring to "light." What's up with that?

IAGO
O, beware, my lord, of jealousy;
It is the green-eyed monster which doth mock
The meat it feeds on; (3.3.15)

Thought: Iago's pretty good at manipulating Othello, don't you think? Here, he pretends to warn Othello not to be a jealous man, pointing out that jealousy ends up destroying the heart of the man who falls prey to it.

OTHELLO
Why, why is this?
Think'st thou I'ld make a life of jealousy,
To follow still the changes of the moon
With fresh suspicions? No; to be once in doubt
Is once to be resolved: exchange me for a goat,
When I shall turn the business of my soul
To such exsufflicate and blown surmises,
Matching thy inference. 'Tis not to make me jealous
To say my wife is fair, feeds well, loves company,
Is free of speech, sings, plays and dances well;
Where virtue is, these are more virtuous:
Nor from mine own weak merits will I draw
The smallest fear or doubt of her revolt;
For she had eyes, and chose me. No, Iago;

I'll see before I doubt; when I doubt, prove;
And on the proof, there is no more but this,—
Away at once with love or jealousy! (3.3.31)

Thought: Here, Othello claims that he won't be destroyed by jealousy. He reasons that Desdemona "had eyes, and chose [him]" despite, presumably, the fact that he is black. But, then, Othello lets slip that he may in fact be a bit more jealous and suspicious of his wife than he lets on – he says he wants some "proof" of Desdemona's infidelity. Looks like Iago's master plan may work out after all.

IAGO
Trifles light as air
Are to the jealous confirmations strong
As proofs of holy writ: this may do something. (3.3.33)

Thought: Iago realizes that real proof of Desdemona's supposed infidelity is not necessary because mere suspicion is enough to feed Othello's jealousy. In the case of Othello, Iago will use the handkerchief Othello gave Desdemona in order to convince Othello that Desdemona's been cheating. (Remember, when Desdemona dropped her handkerchief by accident, Emilia picked it up and gave it to Iago. Iago says he's going to drop it for Cassio to find.) Even though the handkerchief is a mere "trifle, light as air," once Othello sees it in another man's possession, he'll think he has solid proof that Desdemona is unfaithful. When Iago says the handkerchief will be "as proofs of holy writ" to Othello, he means that Othello will see the handkerchief as the *gospel truth* that Desdemona's a cheater.

IAGO
The Moor already changes with my poison.
Dangerous conceits are, in their natures, poisons.
Which at the first are scarce found to distaste,
But with a little act upon the blood.
Burn like the mines of Sulphur. I did say so:
Look, where he comes!
Not poppy, nor mandragora,
Nor all the drowsy syrups of the world,
Shall ever medicine thee to that sweet sleep
Which thou owedst yesterday. (3.3.33)

Thought: Iago realizes the unbelievable power of jealousy. Here, he claims that he has poisoned Othello's mind by suggesting Desdemona may be up to something naughty. Because Iago has succeeded in making Othello suspicious, Othello will never, ever have a good night of sleep again, not even if he used the best sleeping medicine in the world.

EMILIA
Pray heaven it be state-matters, as you think,
And no conception nor no jealous toy
Concerning you.
DESDEMONA
Alas the day! I never gave him cause.
EMILIA
But jealous souls will not be answer'd so;
They are not ever jealous for the cause,
But jealous for they are jealous: 'tis a monster
Begot upon itself, born on itself.
DESDEMONA
Heaven keep that monster from Othello's mind! (3.4.3)

Thought: Emilia understands the nature of jealousy. Here, she points out that jealous husbands like Othello never really need any *cause* to be jealous – they just *are* jealous. What's interesting about this passage is the way Emilia explains that jealousy is like a "monster / begot on itself, born on itself." In other words, jealousy is generated out of nothing and multiplies or reproduces by feeding on itself. Compare Emilia's description of jealousy to what Iago has to say about bringing his "monstrous birth" to light in 1.3.12, above.

DESDEMONA
Where should I lose that handkerchief, Emilia?
EMILIA
I know not, madam.
DESDEMONA
Believe me, I had rather have lost my purse
Full of crusadoes: and, but my noble Moor
Is true of mind and made of no such baseness
As jealous creatures are, it were enough
To put him to ill thinking.
EMILIA
Is he not jealous?
DESDEMONA
Who, he? I think the sun where he was born
Drew all such humours from him. (3.4.7)

Thought: Desdemona is frantic when she discovers she's lost her handkerchief, as it was a meaningful gift from her husband. What's interesting is that poor Desdemona has no idea how her husband will react – she says Othello isn't the jealous type so there's no need to worry. According to her, Othello's "true of mind" and much too "noble" to stoop to "such baseness."

OTHELLO
Speak of me as I am; nothing extenuate,
Nor set down aught in malice: then must you speak
Of one that loved not wisely but too well;
Of one not easily jealous, but being wrought
Perplex'd in the extreme(5.2.341-345)

Thought: Othello begs to be spoken of as a man so "perplex'd" that he didn't know what he was doing when he accused Desdemona of infidelity and murdered her. He doesn't want to be remembered as a man who was "easily jealous." Why is that?

Race Quotes

IAGO
Even now, now, very now, an old black ram
Is tupping your white ewe. Arise, arise;
Awake the snorting citizens with the bell,
Or else the devil will make a grandsire of you.
Arise I say! (1.1.9)

Thought: Iago uses racist slurs when he wakens Brabantio with the news that his daughter, Desdemona (a white Venetian), has eloped with Othello (an older, black man). When Iago says an "old black ram" (Othello) is "tupping" (sleeping with) Brabantio's "white ewe" (Desdemona), he plays on Elizabethan notions that black men have an animal-like, hyper-sexuality. This seems geared at manipulating Brabantio's fears of miscegenation (when a couple "mixes races" through marriage and/or sex).

History Snack: It's also important to note that, although Othello is a Christian, Iago calls him "the devil," playing on a sixteenth century idea that black men were evil and that the devil often took the shape and form of a black man. Check out what Reginald Scott had to say in his famous 1584 book, *The Discovery of Witchcraft*: "Bodin alloweth the divell the shape of a black moore, and as he saith, he used to appear to Mawd Cruse, Kate Darey, and Jon Harviller." (Later, it's no surprise that Brabantio will accuse Othello of using black magic to woo Desdemona.)

BRABANTIO
this is Venice;
My house is not a grange.
[…]
IAGO
Because we come to
do you service and you think we are ruffians, you'll
have your daughter covered with a Barbary horse;
you'll have your nephews neigh to you; you'll have
coursers for cousins and gennets for germans.

[...]
I am one, sir, that comes to tell you your daughter
and the Moor are now making the beast with two backs.
you'll have your daughter covered with a Barbary horse;
you'll have your nephews neigh to you. (1.1.7)

Thought: We've seen how Iago uses animal imagery in his racist diatribe against Othello, which is grounded in the idea that black men (and women) are inhuman. Here, Brabantio objects to Iago's middle-of-the-night assertions that Desdemona has eloped by saying his house isn't a "grange" (a farm or a farmhouse). Iago takes the opportunity to pun on the term "grange," as he claims that Desdemona is having sex with a "barbary horse" and, as a result, Brabantio will have relatives that "neigh to him." Desdemona and Othello, he says, are "making the beast with two backs" (in other words, *humping*, like camels). This isn't the first time Iago has implied that Othello's animal-like sexuality corrupts Desdemona. Compare this to 1.1.9 above.

BRABANTIO
She, in spite of nature,
Of years, of country, credit, every thing,
To fall in love with what she fear'd to look on!
It is a judgment maim'd and most imperfect
That will confess perfection so could err
Against all rules of nature, (1.3.6)

Thought: Desdemona's father argues that her love for Othello is unnatural, since, according to him, Desdemona would never fall for a black man who she "fear'd to look on." Of course, Brabantio couldn't be more wrong about his daughter – Desdemona *is* in love Othello. It seems that Iago has played Brabantio perfectly. Iago knew that Brabantio was racist and, as previous passages demonstrate, he used Brabantio's attitude toward the idea of a mixed marriage in order to rile the man against Othello. Brabantio repeatedly insists that Othello must have "enchanted" Desdemona with "foul charms" and magic spells. Otherwise, he insists, Desdemona never would never have run "to the sooty bosom" of Othello (1.2.2).

DUKE OF VENICE
And, noble signior,
If virtue no delighted beauty lack,
Your son-in-law is far more fair than black.' (1.3.22)

Thought: Not everyone in Venice shares Brabantio's views of Othello. The Senators and the Duke obviously admire Othello, who is a celebrated and honorable military leader. Here, the Duke defends Othello against Brabantio's accusations that Othello used "magic" on Desdemona. On the one hand, we can read the Duke's assertion that Othello is virtuous and "fair" as a compliment. On the other hand, the Duke's words are also troubling because the compliment to Othello hinges on the idea that blackness has negative connotations. Ultimately, the Duke implies that Othello is "fair" *despite* the fact that he is black. This suggests that Othello is the exception to the rule.

Her father loved me; oft invited me;
Still question'd me the story of my life,
From year to year, the battles, sieges, fortunes,
That I have passed.
I ran it through, even from my boyish days,
To the very moment that he bade me tell it;
Wherein I spake of most disastrous chances,
Of moving accidents by flood and field
Of hair-breadth scapes i' the imminent deadly breach,
Of being taken by the insolent foe
And sold to slavery, of my redemption thence
And portance in my travels' history:
Wherein of antres vast and deserts idle,
Rough quarries, rocks and hills whose heads touch heaven
It was my hint to speak,--such was the process;
And of the Cannibals that each other eat,
The Anthropophagi and men whose heads
Do grow beneath their shoulders. This to hear
Would Desdemona seriously incline: (1.3.4)

Thought: Here, Othello explains to the Duke and the Senate how Desdemona fell for him –
when Brabantio would invite Othello to tell stories about his past, Desdemona paid serious
attention and fell in love. This passage is significant for a couple of reasons. First, it reveals that
Brabantio "loved" Othello, so long as Othello was a military hero defending Venice and *not* in a
romantic relationship with his, Brabantio's, daughter. Here's what actor Paul Robeson (the
black American actor who broke the color barrier when he played Othello on Broadway in 1943)
had to say about the play:

"In the Venice of that time [Othello] was in practically the same position as a coloured man in
America today [1930]. He was a general, and while he could be valuable as a fighter he was
tolerated, just as a negro who could save New York from a disaster would become a great man
overnight. So soon, however, as Othello wanted a white woman, Desdemona, everything was
changed, just as New York would be indignant if their coloured man married a white woman."
(See "My Fight for Fame. How Shakespeare Paved My Way to Stardom." *Pearson's Weekly,*
April 5, 1930, p 100.)

We're also interested in the significance of how Othello's stories about travel, adventure, and
even his enslavement lend Othello a romantic and exotic quality that appealed to Desdemona
(and others who listened). Despite the way Othello's stories lend him an exotic air, some
scholars have pointed out that this passage sounds a lot like some stories that were written by
white European travelers. (As we know, Shakespeare lived in an age of exploration, when the
English were enthralled with stories about encounters with new people and cultures. Check out,
for example, _The Voyages and Travels of Sir John Mandeville_, compiled in the fourteenth
century but reprinted in 1582.) Othello, then, seems to present himself here as, well, a white
European traveler, one who has encountered (and lived to tell about) primitive "cannibals" and

"men whose heads do grow beneath their shoulders." Why does Othello do this? Is he trying to distance himself from the kinds of racist stereotypes sixteenth century Europeans assigned to foreigners and black men (savage, animalistic, etc.)?

We also want to point out how the tragedy of *Othello* is that, by play's end, Othello ends up fulfilling a racist stereotype (that black men are savage murderers) when he kills his white wife in her bed. In other words, Othello ends up becoming not unlike the murdering exotics he talks about in his adventure stories. So, what's going on here? Does this mean the play is racist? Or, was Shakespeare trying to provoke his sixteenth-century audiences into (re)thinking their ideas about racial identity?

IAGO
Ay, there's the point: as—to be bold with you—
Not to affect many proposed matches
Of her own clime, complexion, and degree,
Whereto we see in all things nature tends—
Foh! one may smell in such a will most rank,
Foul disproportion thoughts unnatural.
But pardon me. I do not in position
Distinctly speak of her, though I may fear
Her will, recoiling to her better judgment,
May fall to match you with her country forms
And happily repent. (3.3.29)

Thought: Iago suggests that there's something "unnatural" and "rank" about Desdemona if she would decide to marry a black man instead of a man who is of "her own clime, complexion, and degree" (a.k.a. a European man, especially a man from Venice). The word "rank" has serious sexual connotations for Shakespeare – it implies a kind of festering and rot associated with sexually transmitted disease. So, Iago is implying that Desdemona's sexual desire for Othello not only makes her "unnatural," but also suggests that she's promiscuous and corrupt – the kind of girl who might have an STD. (Compare Iago's words here to Hamlet's obsession with his mother's "rank" marriage bed by checking out <u>our discussion of "Symbols" in *Hamlet*</u>.)

We also want to point out that Iago isn't just playing on Othello's fears about his wife's sexuality. Iago also plays on Othello's fears about his status as a black Moor. Iago says Desdemona will eventually change her mind or "repent" for being with him, leaving Othello for a white man instead. Notice Othello doesn't disagree with any of this. It seems Othello's already beginning to believe that Desdemona is or will be unfaithful to him because 1) she's promiscuous and 2) because Othello is a black man and therefore, not good enough for Desdemona. None of what Iago has to say is true. So, why is Othello so easily manipulated by Iago? Is it because Iago tells him what Othello already suspects to be true? If so, does this mean that Othello is a victim of society's racist ideologies?

OTHELLO
My name, that was as fresh
As Dian's visage, is now begrimed and black
As mine own face. (3.3.54)

Thought: This is one of the most important passages in the play. When Othello suspects that Desdemona is cheating on him with Cassio (she's not, by the way), he suggests that his "name," or his reputation, is now soiled and "begrimed" because of his wife's supposed infidelity. (This idea, that a wife's fidelity to her husband can make or break a man's good reputation is pretty common in Shakespeare's plays. See, for example, *The Comedy of Errors*, where the fidelity of Antipholus of Ephesus's wife plays such an important role in her husband's good name around town.)

What's interesting about this passage is Othello's use of a racist discourse. When he says his "name" used to be "as fresh as Dian's" face, he aligns his (former) *good* reputation with the "fresh[ness]" of a *white* face. (Diane is the goddess of the *pale* moon and of chastity.) Now that Othello feels his wife's supposed sexual infidelity has soiled his good reputation, he compares his once good name to his "begrimed and black" face. In other words, Othello associates the blackness of his own skin with something dirty and stained, which is exactly the kind of thing that the racist Venetian characters (like Brabantio) have been saying all along.

The point we're trying to make here is that, by this moment in the play, Othello seems to have internalized the racist ideologies of other characters. He sees himself as a soiled (and soiling) black man.

Note: Some versions of the play read "*Her* name, that was as fresh / as Dian's visage is now begrimed and black / as my own face." How does the substitution of "*her* name" for "*my* name" change the meaning of this passage? (Psst. This is a great paper topic...)

OTHELLO
All my fond love thus do I blow to heaven.
'Tis gone.
Arise, black vengeance, from thy hollow cell! (3.3.63)

Thought: Othello himself associates blackness with something negative – "vengeance."

Yet I'll not shed her blood;
Nor scar that whiter skin of hers than snow,
And smooth as monumental alabaster.
Yet she must die, else she'll betray more men.
Put out the light, and then put out the light:
If I quench thee, thou flaming minister,
I can again thy former light restore. (5.2.1)

Thought: As Othello resolves to kill Desdemona, he is noticeably preoccupied with Desdemona's "whiter" than snow skin. He implies he won't stab her because he doesn't want to "scar" her flesh. He also seems to think of her as a kind of pale statue – her skin's as "smooth as monumental alabaster." What's up with *that*? Why does Othello fixate on Desdemona's skin color (as he contemplates her infidelity) just before he kills her?

OTHELLO
She's, like a liar, gone to burning hell:
'Twas I that kill'd her.
EMILIA
O, the more angel she,
And you the blacker devil! (5.2.36)

Thought: When Othello kills Desdemona, he enacts a racist stereotype – that black men are violent, savage, and to be feared. Does this make the play and/or Shakespeare racist? Or, is there a more complex idea at work in the play?

Speak of me as I am; nothing extenuate,
Nor set down aught in malice: then must you speak
Of one that loved not wisely but too well;
Of one not easily jealous, but being wrought
Perplex'd in the extreme; of one whose hand,
Like the base Indian, threw a pearl away
Richer than all his tribe; of one whose subdued eyes,
Albeit unused to the melting mood,
Drop tears as fast as the Arabian trees
Their medicinal gum.(5.2.68)

Thought: By this point, it's pretty clear that Othello has internalized the racist ideas that were so common in the sixteenth century. When Othello realizes that he murdered Desdemona for no good reason (Desdemona has been faithful and loving all along), he imagines he's just like a "base Indian" who "threw a pearl away" without knowing its true worth. What's interesting about this passage is the way Othello's comparison gives voice to a common notion among Elizabethans – that Native Americans and black Africans alike are "base," or uncivilized. (Accounts of European encounters with Native Americans are full of stories about how Europeans were able to trade worthless beads for precious gems and gold – the idea being that natives were too ignorant to know the "true" value of anything.) It's also worth noting that Othello compares Desdemona to a pearl, a white gem commonly associated with purity.

Gender Quotes
Awake! what, ho, Brabantio! thieves! thieves! thieves!
Look to your house, your daughter and your bags!
Thieves! thieves! (1.1.7)

Thought: Iago's looking to stir up trouble for Othello when he awakens Brabantio with the news that Othello has eloped with Desdemona. But why does he say "thieves" are the problem? As Brabantio's unmarried daughter, Desdemona is basically considered her father's property. Since she's married Othello without dad's permission, Iago suggests that Othello has stolen her from Brabantio. Be sure to also check out Act one, Scene two, where Brabantio shouts at Othello "O thou foul thief, where hast thou stow'd my daughter (1.2.2). Check out our "Quotes" for "Marriage" if you want to think about this some more.

*'Zounds, sir, you're robb'd; for shame, put on
your gown;
Your heart is burst, you have lost half your soul;
Even now, now, very now, an old black ram
Is tupping your white ewe. Arise, arise;
Awake the snorting citizens with the bell,
Or else the devil will make a grandsire of you:
Arise, I say. (1.1.10)*

Thought: There's that reference to Brabantio being "robb'd" again. As we pointed out in the previous passage, Iago suggests that Desdemona's elopement is a kind of theft. What's interesting to us about this passage, however, is that Iago plays on fears of miscegenation (when interracial couples "intermix" via sex and/or marriage) when he says an "old black ram" (Othello) is "tupping" (sleeping with) Brabantio's "white ewe" (Desdemona). (By the way, a "ewe" is a lamb, so there's a suggestion that Desdemona's white skin makes her pure.) Iago's vivid and crude description of the lovemaking between a black man and a white woman is meant to scare Brabantio into thinking that Desdemona's lamb-like purity and whiteness are being contaminated and compromised by her sexual relationship with a black man. Not only that, Iago suggests that Othello is a "devil" that will make Brabantio the "grandsire" of black (like the devil) babies.

*My story being done,
She gave me for my pains a world of sighs:
She swore, in faith, twas strange, 'twas passing strange,
'Twas pitiful, 'twas wondrous pitiful:
She wish'd she had not heard it, yet she wish'd
That heaven had made her such a man: she thank'd me,
And bade me, if I had a friend that loved her,
I should but teach him how to tell my story.
And that would woo her. Upon this hint I spake:
She loved me for the dangers I had pass'd,
And I loved her that she did pity them. (1.2.4)*

Thought: Here, Othello explains that Desdemona fell in love with him while listening to his life stories – romantic tales of travel, adventure, and danger. When Othello recalls that Desdemona said "she wish'd that heaven had made her such a man," we can interpret the line in a couple of ways. On the one hand, it seems pretty obvious that Desdemona wishes heaven "had made

such a man" *for her to marry*, especially given the fact that she suggests that Othello's stories could "woo" her. At the same time, we can read the line to mean that Desdemona wishes heaven had literally *made her a man* (instead of a woman). Desdemona's the kind of girl who craves action and adventure and she's not content to sit at home. Think, for example, of the fact that she'd rather go to war (1.3.2) right along side Othello, who lovingly calls Desdemona his "fair warrior" when she shows up in Cyprus (2.1.1). Bet you're wondering what the heck happens to this bold, adventurous girl between the time she married Othello and the time she rather passively allows her husband to strangle her. Check out our "Character Analysis" of Desdemona if you want to think about this some more.

Look to her, Moor, if thou hast eyes to see:
She has deceived her father, and may thee. (1.3.10)

Thought: Brabantio perpetuates a pretty unfair stereotype of young women in these lines – he suggests that since Desdemona has "deceived her father" by running off to elope with Othello, she'll probably "deceive" her new husband too. The idea is that an unruly daughter will make an unruly and promiscuous wife. Compare this to 3.3.17, below.

IAGO
She did deceive her father, marrying you;
[...]
OTHELLO
And so she did. (3.3.18)

Thought: When Iago wants to make Othello suspect Desdemona's been unfaithful, he suggests a woman who disobeys and "deceive[s] her father is likely to screw around on her husband. Othello's response implies that he feels the same way. Instead of seeing Desdemona's decision to elope with Othello (despite her father's disapproval) as a sign of his wife's loyalty to him, Othello sees Desdemona's willingness to elope as a prelude to her infidelity. It seems that Othello's sexist assumptions leave him pretty vulnerable to Iago's plotting.

Look to your wife; observe her well with Cassio;
Wear your eye thus, not jealous nor secure:
I would not have your free and noble nature,
Out of self-bounty, be abused; look to't:
I know our country disposition well;
In Venice they do let heaven see the pranks
They dare not show their husbands; their best conscience
Is not to leave't undone, but keep't unknown. (3.3.17)

Thought: Iago claims that Venetian women can't be trusted because they all deceive their husbands with their secret "pranks." This seems to be the dominant attitude in the play, wouldn't you say? Just about every male character in the play assumes that women are promiscuous and disloyal. Perhaps this is the reason why Iago is able to manipulate Othello into

believing that Desdemona is unfaithful.

History Snack: In Elizabethan England, Venice was infamous for its courtesans (prostitutes). When Elizabethans thought about Venice, they often imagined it to be a city full of promiscuous women. Check out what Thomas Coryat has to say in his account of his travels to Venice:

[t]he name of a Courtezan of Venice is famoused over all Christendome […] The woman that professeth this trade is called in the Italian tongue Cotezana, which word is derived from the Italian word cortesia that signifieth courtesie. Because these kinds of women are said to receive courtesies of their favorites […] As for the number of these Venetian courtesans it is very great. For it is thought there are of them in the whole city and other adjacent places, as Murano, Malamocco, etc. at the least twenty thousand, whereof many are esteemed so loose that they are said to open their quivers to every arrow, a most ungodly thing without doubt that there should be tolleration of such licentious wantons in so glorious, so potent, so renowned a city." (Coryat's Crudities , 1611)

Now will I question Cassio of Bianca,
A huswife that by selling her desires
Buys herself bread and clothes: it is a creature
That dotes on Cassio; as 'tis the strumpet's plague
To beguile many and be beguiled by one:
He, when he hears of her, cannot refrain
From the excess of laughter. Here he comes: (4.1.19)

Thought: Here, Iago tells the audience that he'll trick Othello into believing that Cassio is bragging about an affair with Desdemona when, in reality, Cassio will be bragging about his relationship with Bianca, a courtesan.

Iago notes that notes Bianca's a "huswife" (or, hussy) who makes a living by forging relationships with men like Cassio. Iago makes some pretty obnoxious assumptions about Bianca. According to Iago, all "strumpets" deceive lots of men but usually end up being deceived (and heartbroken) by the one man they fall in love with. As evidence, Iago refers to the fact that Bianca is in love with Cassio, who doesn't love her back. Instead, Cassio finds her to be "laugh[able]" and makes fun of her when talking with his male friends. Our point? Although Iago accuses courtesans like Bianca of "beguile[ing]" men, this passage seems emblematic of the way the men in the play think nothing of *using* women. Also, Iago's the one doing all the "beguile[ing]" here, isn't he? It seems like Shakespeare's pretty sympathetic toward Bianca and the other women in the play.

OTHELLO
[Striking her] Devil!
DESDEMONA
I have not deserved this.
[…]
OTHELLO

O devil, devil!
If that the earth could teem with woman's tears,
Each drop she falls would prove a crocodile.
Out of my sight!
DESDEMONA
I will not stay to offend you. (4.1.49)

Thought: When we think of *Othello*, our thoughts often turn to Othello's tragic downfall and/or the way he's victimized by Iago. But, here's a reminder that the real victim in the play is Desdemona. At the play's beginning, Desdemona is strong, confident, and defiant but she winds up becoming the victim of Othello's physical and emotional abuse. From this point on, she is passive and obedient and by the play's end, she blames herself for Othello's violent behavior. Later, when Emilia asks Desdemona who has harmed her, Desdemona replies "Nobody; I myself. Farewell" (5.2.29). We can't help but notice that Desdemona exhibits a classic symptom of "battered woman syndrome" – instead of telling Emilia the truth about Othello strangling her, she blames herself (and not her attacker) for the abuse she endures.

But I do think it is their husbands' faults
If wives do fall: say that they slack their duties,
And pour our treasures into foreign laps,
Or else break out in peevish jealousies,
Throwing restraint upon us; or say they strike us,
Or scant our former having in despite;
Why, we have galls, and though we have some grace,
Yet have we some revenge. Let husbands know
Their wives have sense like them: they see and smell
And have their palates both for sweet and sour,
As husbands have. What is it that they do
When they change us for others? Is it sport?
I think it is: and doth affection breed it?
I think it doth: is't frailty that thus errs?
It is so too: and have not we affections,
Desires for sport, and frailty, as men have?
Then let them use us well: else let them know,
The ills we do, their ills instruct us so. (4.3.16)

Thought: After Desdemona naively asks if there are any women who would actually cheat on their husbands, Emilia replies that, yes, there sure are and it's the fault of unkind husbands. According to Emilia, husbands cheat on their wives and often physically abuse them, prompting women to stray. What's more, women have sexual desires, just like men, and women are also "frail" and imperfect, just like some husbands. In other words, Emilia recognizes there's a double standard when it comes to gender and fidelity and she heartily objects.

OK, it's pretty clear Emilia is fed up with men, and who can blame her? She's married to Iago, the biggest jerk in the world. At the same time, however, we wonder why in the world Emilia would be so loyal to Iago if she knows what a creep he is. Why, for example, does she willingly

agree to give Iago Desdemona's handkerchief? She has to know Iago is up to no good, doesn't she? Is Emilia a hypocrite? Or, is she the victim of abuse like Desdemona?

OTHELLO
I had been happy, if the general camp,
Pioners and all, had tasted her sweet body,
So I had nothing known. O, now, for ever
Farewell the tranquil mind! farewell content!
Farewell the plumed troop, and the big wars,
That make ambition virtue! O, farewell!
Farewell the neighing steed, and the shrill trump,
The spirit-stirring drum, the ear-piercing fife,
The royal banner, and all quality,
Pride, pomp and circumstance of glorious war!
And, O you mortal engines, whose rude throats
The immortal Jove's dead clamours counterfeit,
Farewell! Othello's occupation's gone! (3.3.49)

Thought: Because Othello (mistakenly) believes Desdemona has cheated on him, Othello feels like he can't be a soldier any more. All the manly, warlike things – military music, thrusting cannons, and big wars – are denied him; he is convinced that he has lost his masculine, soldier identity. What's up with that? Does he say this because he feels that he has been emasculated? Because he believes that his credibility as a military leader has been compromised? Or, is he suggesting that he is so distraught by Desdemona's supposed affair that he will never find pleasure in the things he once loved (being a military man)? Something else?

OTHELLO
I will chop her into messes: cuckold me! (4.1.187-198)

Thought: Othello is filled with rage at the idea that Desdemona has made him a "cuckold" (a man whose wife has cheated on him). To be a "cuckold" was a shameful thing in Elizabethan society and meant that a husband's masculinity had been destroyed.

OTHELLO
Had it pleased heaven
To try me with affliction; had they rain'd
All kinds of sores and shames on my bare head.
Steep'd me in poverty to the very lips,
Given to captivity me and my utmost hopes,
I should have found in some place of my soul
A drop of patience: but, alas, to make me
A fixed figure for the time of scorn
To point his slow unmoving finger at! (4.2.48-60)

Thought: Othello tells Desdemona that the worst thing about her cheating on him is that it makes him become a ridiculous figure – the cheated-on husband, one that people will just laugh at. (We know, of course, that Othello is wrong about Desdemona's supposed infidelity.) It seems like Othello isn't so much "heartbroken" by the idea that his wife has been unfaithful as he is embarrassed and ashamed.

Sex Quotes

IAGO
Even now, now, very now, an old black ram
Is topping your white ewe. Arise, arise;
Awake the snorting citizens with the bell,
Or else the devil will make a grandsire of you:
…you'll have your daughter covered with a Barbary horse;
you'll have your nephews neigh to you (1.1.)

Thought: In order to manipulate Brabantio's fears of miscegenation, Iago uses animal metaphors to suggest that Desdemona is being defiled by Othello. Check out "Race" for more on this.

IAGO
'Faith, he to-night hath boarded a land carack:
If it prove lawful prize, he's made for ever.
CASSIO
I do not understand.
IAGO
He's married. (1.2.5)

Thought: Iago describes marriage as a violent takeover of an enemy's prize ship. This brings us back to the theory that love is a war in Othello, and Iago is trying to play maestro – or more likely, general.

OTHELLO
Come,
My dear love
The purchase made, the fruits are to ensue:
The profit's yet to come 'tween me and you.
Good night. (2.3.2)

Thought: At this point in the play, Othello talks about sex in positive terms – as a fruit to enjoy, something that "profits" both man and woman. (On the other hand, we could say that Othello's tendency to use financial metaphors – "purchase" and "profit" – make us a little uncomfortable. If marriage is something akin to a "purchase," that leaves the door wide open for viewing one's spouse as a possession.

It's also important to note that it's pretty clear that Desdemona and Othello haven't yet consummated their marriage since Othello says good times in the sack are "yet to come." When Othello says good night to his attendants here, it's obvious that he and Desdemona are running off to have sex, finally. But, shortly thereafter, Othello and Desdemona's evening of fun is interrupted when Cassio gets drunk and gets into a brawl, which Othello is called upon to mediate. So, we're not sure if Othello and Desdemona ever get a chance to do the deed. Why does this matter? Well, some critics argue that the couple never has sex. Other critics argue that they do hook up, which may leave Othello feeling as though he has "contaminated" his wife's sexual and racial purity. After Othello sleeps with his wife, she suddenly becomes a "whore" in Othello's mind. This, according to some, explains why Othello is quick to believe that Desdemona's got something going on the side with Cassio.

OTHELLO
What dost thou say, Iago?
IAGO
Did Michael Cassio, when you woo'd my lady,
Know of your love?
OTHELLO
He did, from first to last: why dost thou ask?
IAGO
But for a satisfaction of my thought;
No further harm.
OTHELLO
Why of thy thought, Iago?
IAGO
I did not think he had been acquainted with her.
OTHELLO
O, yes; and went between us very oft.
IAGO
Indeed!
OTHELLO
Indeed! ay, indeed: discern'st thou aught in that?
Is he not honest? (3.2.14)

Thought: This is where Iago plants the seeds of doubt in Othello's mind. Iago suggests that Cassio, who often acted as a go-between when Othello was wooing Desdemona, "went between" Othello and his girl in more ways than one, wink, wink. Iago doesn't come right and *say* that Cassio and Desdemona have been sneaking around – he *implies* that something's up and Othello takes the bait.

DESDEMONA
Why do you speak so faintly?
Are you not well?
OTHELLO

I have a pain upon my forehead here. (3.3.2)

Thought: After Iago plants the seeds of jealousy in Othello's mind, Othello complains of having a headache, which is a big, big clue that Othello thinks Desdemona's been unfaithful. In sixteenth century literature (Shakespeare's especially), any time a man has a headache or there's some kind of reference to a man having horns growing out of his head, we can be pretty certain there's a reference being made to cuckoldry. A "cuckold" is a man who has been cheated on by his wife, and "cuckolds" are frequently portrayed as having horns. This is why Othello says that married men are "fated" to suffer the "forked plague" (3.3.42) just a few lines earlier.

OTHELLO
My name, that was as fresh
As Dian's visage, is now begrimed and black
As mine own face. (3.3.54)

Thought: We talk about this passage in more detail in "Race," but it's worth mentioning in our discussion here as well. When Othello suspects that Desdemona is cheating on him with Cassio, he suggests that his "name," or his reputation, is now soiled and "begrimed" because of his wife's supposed infidelity. This idea, that a wife's fidelity to her husband can make or break a man's good reputation is pretty common in Shakespeare's plays. See, for example, *The Comedy of Errors*, where the fidelity of Antipholus of Ephesus's wife plays such an important role in her husband's good name around town.

OTHELLO
Give me a living reason she's disloyal.
IAGO
I do not like the office:
But, sith I am enter'd in this cause so far,
Prick'd to't by foolish honesty and love,
I will go on. I lay with Cassio lately;
And, being troubled with a raging tooth,
I could not sleep.
There are a kind of men so loose of soul,
That in their sleeps will mutter their affairs:
One of this kind is Cassio:
In sleep I heard him say 'Sweet Desdemona,
Let us be wary, let us hide our loves;'
And then, sir, would he gripe and wring my hand,
Cry 'O sweet creature!' and then kiss me hard,
As if he pluck'd up kisses by the roots
That grew upon my lips: then laid his leg
Over my thigh, and sigh'd, and kiss'd; and then
Cried 'Cursed fate that gave thee to the Moor!'
OTHELLO

O monstrous! monstrous!
(3.3.56)

Thought: When Othello asks for "living reason" (proof) that Desdemona's been "disloyal," Iago tells him about a sexy dream that Cassio supposedly had one night while he was lying in bed next to Iago (presumably, at an army camp). According to Iago, Cassio talked in his sleep while having a naughty dream about Desdemona. Not only that, but Cassio also grabbed Iago, wrapped his leg over his thigh, and made out with him (all while dreaming about Desdemona).

What's going on here? First, it's important to note that Iago is framing Cassio to make it look like he's sleeping with Desdemona. Second, Othello seems willing to accept this story as "proof" that Desdemona's cheating. Third, Iago is describing a blatantly homoerotic moment he has allegedly shared with Cassio, which begs the following question: Is Othello upset/jealous that Cassio (allegedly) had a dream about his wife or, that Cassio was lying in bed and groping Iago? Literary critics have argued both ways, so take your pick and keep reading…

OTHELLO
In the due reverence of a sacred vow
I here engage my words.
IAGO
Do not rise yet.
Kneels
Witness, you ever-burning lights above,
You elements that clip us round about,
Witness that here Iago doth give up
The execution of his wit, hands, heart,
To wrong'd Othello's service! Let him command,
And to obey shall be in me remorse,
What bloody business ever.
[…]
IAGO
I am your own for ever. (3.4.64)

Thought: Now this is interesting. When Othello makes Iago his new lieutenant and Iago vows to kill Cassio, the pair make a pact that looks and sounds a whole lot like a sixteenth-century marriage ceremony. What's up with that? Is this evidence, as some critics suggest, of a homoerotic attachment between Othello and Iago? If so, has Iago wanted all along to displace Desdemona and become Othello's intimate partner?

But I do think it is their husbands' faults
If wives do fall: say that they slack their duties,
And pour our treasures into foreign laps,
Or else break out in peevish jealousies,
Throwing restraint upon us; or say they strike us,
Or scant our former having in despite;

Why, we have galls, and though we have some grace,
Yet have we some revenge. Let husbands know
Their wives have sense like them: they see and smell
And have their palates both for sweet and sour,
As husbands have. What is it that they do
When they change us for others? Is it sport?
I think it is: and doth affection breed it?
I think it doth: is't frailty that thus errs?
It is so too: and have not we affections,
Desires for sport, and frailty, as men have?
Then let them use us well: else let them know,
The ills we do, their ills instruct us so. (4.3.16)

Thought: According to Emilia, husbands cheat on their wives and often physically abuse them, prompting women to stray. What's more, women have sexual desires, just like men, and women are also "frail" and imperfect, just like some husbands. In other words, Emilia recognizes there's a double standard when it comes to gender and fidelity and she heartily objects.

Behold, I have a weapon;
A better never did itself sustain
Upon a soldier's thigh: (5.2.55)

Thought: After Othello strangles Desdemona (for her alleged adultery) on the bed the couple shares, Othello's reference to his "weapon," which rests upon his "soldier's thigh," seems blatantly phallic, don't you think? Othello's words forge a disturbing relationship between sex and death.

Marriage Quotes

O thou foul thief, where hast thou stow'd my daughter. (1.2.2)

Thought: When Brabantio confronts Othello for eloping with Desdemona (without his permission), he accuses his new son-in-law of being a "foul thief," as if Desdemona is piece of property that has been unlawfully taken away from him. We see this same attitude earlier in the play when Iago awakens Brabantio in the middle of the night proclaiming loudly "Awake! what, ho, Brabantio! thieves! thieves! thieves! / Look to your house, your daughter and your bags! / Thieves! thieves!" (1.1.7). What's up with that?

History Snack: It turns out that it's pretty common in Shakespeare's plays (and sixteenth-to-seventeenth-century England in general) for daughters to be considered their father's property – unmarried women are often portrayed as something to be stolen, bartered for and/or traded by men. In *Taming of the Shrew*, for example, when Baptista Minola bargains with his daughter's suitor, he treats Bianca like a possession and even refers to himself as a "merchant" who is undertaking a risky business deal (*Taming of the Shrew*, 2.1.22).

Damn'd as thou art, thou hast enchanted her;
For I'll refer me to all things of sense,
If she in chains of magic were not bound,
Whether a maid so tender, fair and happy,
So opposite to marriage that she shunned
The wealthy curled darlings of our nation,
Would ever have, to incur a general mock,
Run from her guardage to the sooty bosom
Of such a thing as thou, to fear, not to delight.
Judge me the world, if 'tis not gross in sense
That thou hast practised on her with foul charms,
Abused her delicate youth with drugs or minerals
That weaken motion: (1.2.2)

Thought: Brabantio insists that Othello must have "enchanted" Desdemona – why else, asks Brabantio, would she run away from all the (white) eligible bachelors in Venice into the "sooty bosom" of the "Moor"? (Pretty obnoxious, wouldn't you say?) Brabantio's objection to his daughter's marriage to a black man gives voice to fears of miscegenation (when interracial couples marry/have sex, etc., resulting in "mixed race" children).

IAGO
I hate the Moor:
And it is thought abroad, that 'twixt my sheets
He has done my office: I know not if't be true;
But I, for mere suspicion in that kind,
Will do as if for surety. (1.3.12)

Thought: We discuss this passage in "Jealousy," but it's important to the theme of "Marriage" as well. Here, Iago suggests that his wife, Emilia, has cheated on him with Othello. Now, we know this is completely untrue. What we don't know is whether or not Iago actually *believes* that Othello has slept with Emilia. As we know, Iago lists multiple (and incompatible) motives for seeking to destroy Othello (elsewhere, he says he hates Othello because he was passed up for a promotion), so it's entirely possible that Iago's the one who makes up the rumor about Othello and Emilia. On the other hand, most men in the play assume that all women are promiscuous and unfaithful in general, so it's not so surprising that Iago would believe Emilia has been untrue.

IAGO
Now, I do love her too;
Not out of absolute lust, though peradventure
I stand accountant for as great a sin,
But partly led to diet my revenge,
For that I do suspect the lusty Moor
Hath leap'd into my seat; the thought whereof
Doth, like a poisonous mineral, gnaw my inwards;

And nothing can or shall content my soul
Till I am even'd with him, wife for wife,
Or failing so, yet that I put the Moor
At least into a jealousy so strong
That judgment cannot cure. Which thing to do,
If this poor trash of Venice, whom I trash
For his quick hunting, stand the putting on,
I'll have our Michael Cassio on the hip,
Abuse him to the Moor in the rank garb—
For I fear Cassio with my night-cap too— (2.1.22)

Thought: Iago is completely obsessed with infidelity. Earlier, we heard him say that he suspects Othello has slept with Emilia (a sentiment he repeats in this passage). Not only that, he also says he "fear[s]" that even Cassio is sleeping with his wife. What's Iago going to do about it? Why, he's going to try to sleep with Desdemona, which will allow him to get even with the "lusty Moor." If he can't do that, he wants to make Othello believe that Desdemona is screwing around with Cassio.

IAGO
She did deceive her father, marrying you;
[…]
OTHELLO
And so she did. (3.3.18)

Thought: When Iago wants to make Othello suspect Desdemona's been unfaithful, he suggests a woman who disobeys and "deceive[s] her father is likely to screw around on her husband. Othello's response implies that he feels the same way. Instead of seeing Desdemona's decision to elope with Othello (despite her father's disapproval) as a sign of his wife's loyalty to him, Othello sees Desdemona's willingness to elope as a prelude to her infidelity. It seems that Othello's sexist assumptions leave him pretty vulnerable to Iago's plotting.

OTHELLO
O curse of marriage,
That we can call these delicate creatures ours,
And not their appetites! I had rather be a toad,
And live upon the vapour of a dungeon,
Than keep a corner in the thing I love
For others' uses. Yet, 'tis the plague of great ones;
Prerogatived are they less than the base;
'Tis destiny unshunnable, like death:
Even then this forked plague is fated to us
When we do quicken. (3.3.42)

Thought: Get your highlighter out because this is important. When Othello is convinced (by Iago) that Desdemona has cheated on him, he reveals something pretty interesting about himself. It seems that Othello believes all men, both "great" and "base," are "destin[ed]" to be cuckolds. FYI: A "cuckold" is a man whose been cheated on by his wife – cuckolds are commonly associated with horns, which is why Othello refers to cuckoldry as a "forked plague" that men suffer from.

So, if Othello believes that all men are destined, from the moment of their birth, to be cheated on by their wives, then this helps to explain why Othello is so easily convinced that Desdemona has been unfaithful, despite the fact that Iago never actually shows Othello any real evidence.

OTHELLO
What sense had I of her stol'n hours of lust?
I saw't not, thought it not, it harm'd not me:
I slept the next night well, was free and merry;
I found not Cassio's kisses on her lips:
He that is robb'd, not wanting what is stol'n,
Let him not know't, and he's not robb'd at all. (3.3.48)

Thought: In this passage, Othello tries to come to terms with Desdemona's alleged affair with Cassio. In doing so, he voices a pretty common desire among victims of infidelity – he says he'd be much better off if he just didn't *know* about it.

What's most interesting to us about this passage, however, is the way Othello uses the language of theft to describe Desdemona's supposed betrayal. When Othello laments the affair, he suggests that he's been "robb'd" by Cassio. Hmm. This sounds a whole lot like Brabantio's reaction to the news that Desdemona eloped with Othello (see 1.2.2 above), don't you think? When Othello (and Brabantio) say that Desdemona is something that has been "robb'd" or "stol'n" from them, they talk about her as if she's a piece of property that passes from one man to the next.

EMILIA
I am glad I have found this napkin:
This was her first remembrance from the Moor:
My wayward husband hath a hundred times
Woo'd me to steal it; but she so loves the token,
For he conjured her she should ever keep it,
That she reserves it evermore about her
To kiss and talk to. I'll have the work ta'en out,
And give't Iago: what he will do with it
Heaven knows, not I;
I nothing but to please his fantasy. (3.3.1)

Thought: Why does Emilia steal Desdemona's handkerchief and give it to her jerk of a husband, Iago? (She has to know Iago is up to no good, doesn't she?) It seems that, despite (or perhaps because of) Iago's abuse, Emilia still craves her husband's love and approval, which is why she'll stoop to anything in order to "please" him. Check out our "Character" analysis of "Emilia" for more about Emilia's motives.

Minion, your dear lies dead,
And your unblest fate hies: strumpet, I come.
Forth of my heart those charms, thine eyes, are blotted;
Thy bed, lust-stain'd, shall with lust's blood be spotted. (5.1.3)

Thought: Because Othello believes Desdemona has been cheating on him, he rationalizes (in the most irrational and disturbing way) that it's fitting for him to kill his wife on the bed they share as a married couple.

EMILIA
O, who hath done this deed?
DESDEMONA
Nobody; I myself. Farewell
Commend me to my kind lord: O, farewell! (5.2.29)

Thought: When Emilia asks Desdemona who has harmed her, Desdemona blames herself instead of holding Othello accountable. As we know, this isn't the first time Desdemona has been abused by her husband, who accuses her of cheating on him, slaps her in public, and calls her a "whore" – actions that culminate in Othello murdering Desdemona. We can't help but notice that Desdemona exhibits a classic symptom of "battered woman syndrome" – instead of telling Emilia the truth about Othello strangling her, she blames herself (and not her attacker) for the abuse she endures.

Manipulation Quotes

Call up her father,
Rouse him: make after him, poison his delight,
Proclaim him in the streets; incense her kinsmen,
And, though he in a fertile climate dwell,
Plague him with flies: though that his joy be joy,
Yet throw such changes of vexation on't,
As it may lose some colour. (1.1.5)

Thought: Yikes. When Iago talks about corrupting Brabantio's opinion of his fair daughter, Desdemona, he uses the language of poison and plague, which seems pretty appropriate given the nature of Iago's manipulation. When Iago tattles on Othello and Desdemona for eloping, he capitalizes on Brabantio's xenophobic attitude toward mixed race marriages. Here's what Iago says to get Brabantio riled up against Othello:

Even now, now, very now, an old black ram
Is topping your white ewe. Arise, arise;
Awake the snorting citizens with the bell,
Or else the devil will make a grandsire of you:
Arise, I say. (1.1.9)

Check out "Race" if you want to think about the implications of this.

BRABANTIO
O thou foul thief, where hast thou stow'd my daughter?
Damn'd as thou art, thou hast enchanted her;
For I'll refer me to all things of sense,
If she in chains of magic were not bound,
Whether a maid so tender, fair and happy,
So opposite to marriage that she shunned
The wealthy curled darlings of our nation,
Would ever have, to incur a general mock,
Run from her guardage to the sooty bosom
Of such a thing as thou, to fear, not to delight.
Judge me the world, if 'tis not gross in sense
That thou hast practised on her with foul charms,
Abused her delicate youth with drugs or minerals
That weaken motion: I'll have't disputed on;
'Tis probable and palpable to thinking.
I therefore apprehend and do attach thee
For an abuser of the world, a practiser
Of arts inhibited and out of warrant. (1.2.2)

Thought: Brabantio argues that Othello could not have truly won Desdemona's love – it had to be through some kind of trickery or manipulation. Brabantio couldn't be more wrong, of course.

But for my sport and profit. I hate the Moor:
And it is thought abroad, that 'twixt my sheets
He has done my office: I know not if't be true;
But I, for mere suspicion in that kind,
Will do as if for surety. (1.3.12)

Thought: Iago cites multiple and incompatible motives for wanting to destroy Othello. Earlier, he said he hates Othello because "the Moor" passed him over for a promotion but, here, he tells us he hates "the Moor" because he's heard a rumor that Othello has been hooking up with Iago's wife, Emilia, "twixt [Iago's] sheets." It's just not clear whether or not we, as an audience, can believe anything Iago has to say.

SAILOR
The Turkish preparation makes for Rhodes;
So was I bid report here to the state
By Signior Angelo.
[...]
DUKE OF VENICE
Nay, in all confidence, he's not for Rhodes.
[...]
MESSENGER
Of thirty sail: and now they do restem
Their backward course, bearing with frank appearance
Their purposes toward Cyprus. (1.3.2)

Thought: The deception the Turkish navy attempts – appearing as though they are going to attack Rhodes, when actually they want Cyprus – parallels the sneakier, interpersonal deceptions going on in the play. For more about the relationship between literal war and the psychological battle Iago wages against Othello, check out "Quotes" for "Warfare."

BRABANTIO
Look to her, Moor, if thou hast eyes to see:
She has deceived her father, and may thee. (1.3.10)

Thought: Brabantio suggests that, because Desdemona deceived her father when she eloped with Othello, Desdemona will likely deceive her husband. Desdemona, as we know, is completely faithful to Othello. The problem is that Othello seems to buy into the stereotype that unruly daughters make for unruly and promiscuous wives, which is part of the reason why Iago is able to manipulate him so easily. (Later, in Act 3, Scene 3, when Iago echoes Brabantio's point, Othello agrees.) Shakespeare seems to be critiquing this unfair attitude toward women in the play – Othello's distrust in his wife leads to a terrible tragedy when he murders Desdemona.

Virtue! a fig! 'tis in ourselves that we are thus
or thus. Our bodies are our gardens, to the which
our wills are gardeners: so that if we will plant
nettles, or sow lettuce, set hyssop and weed up
thyme, supply it with one gender of herbs, or
distract it with many, either to have it sterile
with idleness, or manured with industry, why, the
power and corrigible authority of this lies in our
wills. (1.3.5)

Thought: When Iago makes an analogy between gardening and exercising free will, we're reminded of the way that Iago is the ultimate *master gardener*, so to speak. Part of what makes him such a brilliant manipulator of Othello is his ability to *plant the seeds* of doubt and jealousy in Othello's mind.

If I can fasten but one cup upon him,
With that which he hath drunk to-night already,
He'll be as full of quarrel and offence
As my young mistress' dog. (2.3.9)

Thought: Iago schemes to get Cassio drunk because he knows Cassio, who is kind of a mean drunk, will end up getting into a fight. Why? Because he wants Cassio (a soldier) to get in trouble with Othello (Cassio's boss/general) so that Desdemona will try to intervene on Cassio's behalf, which will make Othello jealous and suspicious. If this sounds overly elaborate and unrealistic to you, you're not alone. Literary critics often point out that much of Iago's plotting is, well, pretty implausible.

IAGO
Ha! I like not that.
OTHELLO
What dost thou say?
IAGO
Nothing, my lord: or if--I know not what.
OTHELLO
Was not that Cassio parted from my wife?
IAGO
Cassio, my lord! No, sure, I cannot think it,
That he would steal away so guilty-like,
Seeing you coming.
OTHELLO
I do believe 'twas he. (2.3.1)

Thought: Gosh. Iago is an evil genius, don't you think? After watching Desdemona and Cassio chit-chat from afar, Iago suggests that something naughty is going on between Cassio and Othello's wife. He never comes right out and says, "Hey Othello, look at your wife flirt with Cassio," but he *implies* there's something tawdry happening and then acts all innocent when Othello presses the point.

OTHELLO
Get me some poison, Iago; this night: I'll not
expostulate with her, lest her body and beauty
unprovide my mind again: this night, Iago.
IAGO
Do it not with poison, strangle her in her bed, even
the bed she hath contaminated.
OTHELLO
Good, good: the justice of it pleases: very good. (4.1.38)

Thought: Whoa. We know that Iago is out to destroy Othello, but why is he so intent on destroying *Desdemona*? After convincing Othello that Desdemona has been cheating, he manipulates Othello into strangling Desdemona "in her bed." What's up with that? More importantly, what's up with Othello thinking that killing his wife in her bed is "just"? By this point in the play, Othello's mind has been completely warped.

Demand me nothing: what you know, you know:
From this time forth I never will speak word. (5.2.11)

Thought: This is the last time Iago speaks in the play. After Othello demands to know why Iago set out to destroy him, Iago remains silent. But why? One would think that Iago would want to gloat but he refuses to explain his actions, leaving Othello *and the audience* pretty clueless about Iago's motives.

Warfare Quotes

Despise me, if I do not. Three great ones of the city,
In personal suit to make me his lieutenant,
Off-capp'd to him: and, by the faith of man,
I know my price, I am worth no worse a place:
But he; as loving his own pride and purposes,
Evades them, with a bombast circumstance
Horribly stuff'd with epithets of war;
And, in conclusion,
Nonsuits my mediators; for, 'Certes,' says he,
'I have already chose my officer.'
And what was he?
Forsooth, a great arithmetician,
One Michael Cassio, a Florentine,
A fellow almost damn'd in a fair wife;
That never set a squadron in the field,
Nor the division of a battle knows
More than a spinster; unless the bookish theoric,
Wherein the toged consuls can propose
As masterly as he: mere prattle, without practise,
Is all his soldiership. (1.1.2)

Thought: Iago claims that he hates Othello because Othello passed him over for a promotion and chose Michael Cassio as a lieutenant instead. Iago also says that Cassio doesn't know any more about warfare than a housewife or a spinster does – he's never been on the battlefield and his knowledge of war is more "bookish" than experiential. This passage speaks to the way warfare is considered a man's realm (women didn't participate in battle). It also raises the question of *why* Iago hates Othello so much – Othello's refusal to promote Iago is just one of *several* reasons Iago gives for setting out to destroy the general.

Though I do hate him as I do hell-pains.
Yet, for necessity of present life,
I must show out a flag and sign of love,
Which is indeed but sign. (1.1.12)

Thought: After stirring up trouble for Othello with Brabantio, Iago says he needs to get lost because it wouldn't look right for him to be present when his general is confronted by Desdemona's father. For now, Iago says he needs to pretend he loves Othello. What's interesting to us about this passage is the way Iago uses the language of war to describe his relationship with Othello – he'll "show out a flag" as a sign of his loyalty (kind of like waving a peace sign when you have every intention of attacking your enemy). Although Iago is an ensign (the lowest rank of commissioned officers), he acts more like a brilliant general as he wages psychological warfare against Othello throughout the play.

OTHELLO
The tyrant custom, most grave senators,
Hath made the flinty and steel couch of war
My thrice-driven bed of down: I do agnise
A natural and prompt alacrity
I find in hardness, and do undertake
These present wars against the Ottomites.
Most humbly therefore bending to your state,
I crave fit disposition for my wife.
Due reference of place and exhibition,
With such accommodation and besort
As levels with her breeding. (1.3.5)

Thought: Without hesitation, Othello puts aside his new bride to dash off to the war, which seems to suggest that he values his position in the military above his love. On the other hand, we could also point out how Othello goes out of his way to make sure his new wife will be taken care of while he's away.

DESDEMONA
That I did love the Moor to live with him,
My downright violence and storm of fortunes
May trumpet to the world: my heart's subdued
Even to the very quality of my lord:
I saw Othello's visage in his mind,
And to his honour and his valiant parts
Did I my soul and fortunes consecrate.
So that, dear lords, if I be left behind,
A moth of peace, and he go to the war,
The rites for which I love him are bereft me,
And I a heavy interim shall support
By his dear absence. Let me go with him. (1.3.2)

Thought: Desdemona doesn't want to remain behind while her new husband runs off to Cyprus to fight against the Turks. For one thing, she loves Othello and simply wants to be with him. But, it's also important to note that Desdemona seems drawn to the action and adventure of warfare, which is a realm that's only available to men. Check out "Quotes" for "Gender" if you want to know about Desdemona's desire to be a warrior.

OTHELLO
Let her have your voices.
Vouch with me, heaven, I therefore beg it not,
To please the palate of my appetite,
Nor to comply with heat—the young affects
In me defunct—and proper satisfaction.
But to be free and bounteous to her mind:
And heaven defend your good souls, that you think
I will your serious and great business scant
For she is with me: no, when light-wing'd toys
Of feather'd Cupid seal with wanton dullness
My speculative and officed instruments,
That my disports corrupt and taint my business,
Let housewives make a skillet of my helm,
And all indign and base adversities
Make head against my estimation! (1.3.7)

Thought: Othello is concerned that people will think him unprofessional or distracted by love. He assures everybody that love will not get in the way of war, as he has his priorities straight.

OTHELLO
Come, Desdemona: I have but an hour
Of love, of worldly matters and direction,
To spend with thee: we must obey the time. (1.3.10)

Thought: Because Othello is called off to war soon after he elopes with Desdemona, the couple must cram their "honeymoon" into one hour.

OTHELLO
Come, let us to the castle.
News, friends; our wars are done, the Turks
are drown'd.
How does my old acquaintance of this isle?
Honey, you shall be well desired in Cyprus;
I have found great love amongst them. O my sweet,
I prattle out of fashion, and I dote
In mine own comforts. I prithee, good Iago,
Go to the bay and disembark my coffers:

Bring thou the master to the citadel;
He is a good one, and his worthiness
Does challenge much respect. Come, Desdemona,
Once more, well met at Cyprus. (2.1.4)

Thought: After a storm destroys the Turks' ships and the big war is cancelled, Othello is overjoyed to see his "fair warrior," Desdemona. He "prattle[s]" on (rather sweetly) until he catches himself and quickly returns to business.

OTHELLO
All's well now, sweeting; come away to bed.
Sir, for your hurts, myself will be your surgeon:
Lead him off.
Iago, look with care about the town,
And silence those whom this vile brawl distracted.
Come, Desdemona: 'tis the soldiers' life
To have their balmy slumbers waked with strife. (2.3.236-242)

Thought: Once again, Othello's lovemaking has been interrupted by fighting (after Iago gets Cassio drunk and Cassio gets into a brawl, Othello is called upon to settle the matter). At this point, Othello seems resigned to the fact that such interruptions are par for the course when one is a military general.

OTHELLO
Behold, I have a weapon;
A better never did itself sustain
Upon a soldier's thigh: I have seen the day,
That, with this little arm and this good sword,
I have made my way through more impediments
Than twenty times your stop: but, O vain boast! (5.2.55)

Thought: After Othello strangles Desdemona (for her alleged adultery) on the bed the couple shares, Othello's reference to his "weapon," which rests upon his "soldier's thigh," seems blatantly phallic, don't you think? Othello's words forge a disturbing relationship between sex and death.

OTHELLO
Soft you; a word or two before you go.
I have done the state some service, and they know't.
No more of that. I pray you, in your letters,
When you shall these unlucky deeds relate,
Speak of me as I am; nothing extenuate,
Nor set down aught in malice: then must you speak
Of one that loved not wisely but too well;

Of one not easily jealous, but being wrought
Perplex'd in the extreme; of one whose hand,
Like the base Indian, threw a pearl away
Richer than all his tribe; of one whose subdued eyes,
Albeit unused to the melting mood,
Drop tears as fast as the Arabian trees
Their medicinal gum. Set you down this;
And say besides, that in Aleppo once,
Where a malignant and a turban'd Turk
Beat a Venetian and traduced the state,
I took by the throat the circumcised dog,
And smote him, thus. [kills himself] […]
(5.2.66)

Thought: Here, Othello says he "loved" Desdemona "too well" (too much), which suggests that he doesn't really understand the implications of what he's done. We're also interested in the way Othello wants to control the way people think of him (after his death). He wants to be remembered as a soldier who "has done the state some service" and who has killed a lot of Venice's enemies. Yet, he also seems to think of his murder of Desdemona as a crime against the Venetian state, as he compares himself to a "turban'd Turk" by killing himself with the same sword he has used to smite Venice's enemies on the battlefield.

Hate Quotes

IAGO
Though I do hate him as I do hell's pains
Yet for necessity of present life,
I must show out a flag and sign of love,
Which is indeed but sign. (1.1.152-155)
IAGO
I hate the Moor:
And it is thought abroad, that 'twixt my sheets
He has done my office: I know not if't be true;
But I, for mere suspicion in that kind,
Will do as if for surety. (1.3.379-383)

Thought: Iago says his hatred of Othello is based on jealousy.

IAGO
Now, I do love her too;
Not out of absolute lust, though peradventure
I stand accountant for as great a sin,
But partly led to diet my revenge,
For that I do suspect the lusty Moor
Hath leap'd into my seat; the thought whereof

Doth, like a poisonous mineral, gnaw my inwards;
And nothing can or shall content my soul
Till I am even'd with him, wife for wife,
Or failing so, yet that I put the Moor
At least into a jealousy so strong
That judgment cannot cure. Which thing to do,
If this poor trash of Venice, whom I trash
For his quick hunting, stand the putting on,
I'll have our Michael Cassio on the hip,
Abuse him to the Moor in the rank garb—
For I fear Cassio with my night-cap too— (2.1.280-291)

Thought: Yet here, Iago's hatred is rooted in his suspicion that Othello was sleeping with his wife.

MONTANO
And 'tis great pity that the noble Moor
Should hazard such a place as his own second
With one of an ingraft infirmity:
It were an honest action to say
So to the Moor.
IAGO
Not I, for this fair island
I do love Cassio well; and would do much
To cure him of this evil—But, hark! what noise? (2.3.125-136)

Thought: Iago speaks of loving Cassio in the same terms he often speaks of loving Othello; we suspect, then, that he hates Cassio, as he also hates Othello.

OTHELLO
Ay, let her rot, and perish, and be damned to-night;
for she shall not live: no, my heart is turned to
stone; I strike it, and it hurts my hand. O, the
world hath not a sweeter creature: she might lie by
an emperor's side and command him tasks. (4.1.174-178)

Thought: Iago transforms the passion of Othello's love into hatred.

Identity Quotes

For sir, it is as sure as you are Roderigo,
Were I the Moor, I would not be Iago.
In following him, I follow but myself.
Heaven is my judge, not I for love and duty,

But seeming so for my particular end.
For when my outward action doth demonstrate
The native act and figure of my heart
In complement extern, 'tis not long after
But I will wear my heart upon my sleeve
For daws to peck at. I am not what I am. (1.1.4)

Thought: Iago is all about not revealing his true identity or intentions to anyone. Here, he tells Roderigo that he'll never allow his "outward action[s]" to show what's really going on inside of him because that would leave him vulnerable, kind of like allowing birds ("daws") to peck at his "heart." When Iago says "I am not what I am," he cryptically suggests that he's not what he appears to be. This phrase, we should point out, is an inversion of God's line, "I am what I am" (Exodus 3.14), which is in keeping with the play's alignment of Iago with the devil.

It is too true an evil: gone she is;
And what's to come of my despised time
Is nought but bitterness. Now, Roderigo,
Where didst thou see her? O unhappy girl!
With the Moor, say'st thou? Who would be a father!
How didst thou know 'twas she? O she deceives me
Past thought! What said she to you? Get more tapers:
Raise all my kindred. Are they married, think you?
[…]
O heaven! How got she out? O treason of the blood!
Fathers, from hence trust not your daughters' minds
By what you see them act. (1.1.12)

Thought: When Brabantio learns that Desdemona has run off with Othello, he cries out, "Who would be a father!" and wonders "what's to come" of himself. Clearly, Brabantio feels as though his identity as a father and an authority figure have been compromised by Desdemona's elopement, which he interprets as "treason of the blood."

OTHELLO
Let him do his spite:
My services which I have done the signiory
Shall out-tongue his complaints. 'Tis yet to know,—
Which, when I know that boasting is an honour,
I shall promulgate—I fetch my life and being
From men of royal siege, and my demerits
May speak unbonneted to as proud a fortune
As this that I have reach'd: for know, Iago,
But that I love the gentle Desdemona,
I would not my unhoused free condition
Put into circumscription and confine
For the sea's worth. (1.2.2)

Thought: At this point in the play, Othello is so secure in his value to the state of Venice that he says he does not care if Brabantio slanders him. Othello knows he's done nothing wrong in marrying Desdemona and that the Duke will support him, especially since Othello's a decorated war hero. What's interesting about this passage is how it reveals Othello's sense of himself as a military leader – his valuable "services" to the state of Venice have made him an "insider." At the same time, however, we know that Othello is also an "outsider" – he's a foreigner and his skin is black, which leaves him vulnerable to racist attitudes (like Brabantio's) in Venice.

OTHELLO
Most potent, grave, and reverend signiors,
My very noble and approved good masters,
That I have ta'en away this old man's daughter,
It is most true; true, I have married her:
The very head and front of my offending
Hath this extent, no more. Rude am I in my speech,
And little bless'd with the soft phrase of peace:
For since these arms of mine had seven years' pith,
Till now some nine moons wasted, they have used
Their dearest action in the tented field,
And little of this great world can I speak,
More than pertains to feats of broil and battle,
And therefore little shall I grace my cause
In speaking for myself. Yet, by your gracious patience,
I will a round unvarnish'd tale deliver
Of my whole course of love; what drugs, what charms,
What conjuration and what mighty magic,
For such proceeding I am charged withal,
I won his daughter. (1.3.1)

Thought: Othello identifies himself with the roughness of the battlefield, in contrast to the gentleness or sophistication of civilized Venice when he says his "speech" is "rude" and he's not been "bless'd with the soft phrase of peace." Yet, Othello knows darn well that he *is* quite eloquent, as he demonstrates here in an incredibly well-wrought speech that he delivers as a defense of his marriage to Desdemona.

BRABANTIO A maiden never bold;
Of spirit so still and quiet, that her motion
Blush'd at herself; and she, in spite of nature,
Of years, of country, credit, every thing,
To fall in love with what she fear'd to look on!
It is a judgment maim'd and most imperfect
That will confess perfection so could err
Against all rules of nature, and must be driven
To find out practises of cunning hell,
Why this should be. I therefore vouch again

That with some mixtures powerful o'er the blood,
Or with some dram conjured to this effect,
He wrought upon her. (1.3.6)

Thought: Brabantio doesn't seem to know his daughter at all, especially when he claims she is "never bold" and that she "fear'd to look on" Othello. As we know, Desdemona *is* bold – she runs off with a man her father doesn't approve of and defends her actions when confronted by Brabantio and the Venetian court.

OTHELLO
Her father loved me; oft invited me;
Still question'd me the story of my life,
From year to year, the battles, sieges, fortunes,
That I have passed.
I ran it through, even from my boyish days,
To the very moment that he bade me tell it;
Wherein I spake of most disastrous chances,
Of moving accidents by flood and field
Of hair-breadth scapes i' the imminent deadly breach,
Of being taken by the insolent foe
And sold to slavery, of my redemption thence
And portance in my travels' history:
Wherein of antres vast and deserts idle,
Rough quarries, rocks and hills whose heads touch heaven
It was my hint to speak,—such was the process;
And of the Cannibals that each other eat,
The Anthropophagi and men whose heads
Do grow beneath their shoulders. This to hear
Would Desdemona seriously incline:
But still the house-affairs would draw her thence:
Which ever as she could with haste dispatch,
She'ld come again, and with a greedy ear
Devour up my discourse: (1.3.4)

Thought: Othello presents himself as an exotic, exciting person who has travelled the world and seen "Cannibals," "Anthropophagi" (man eaters), and "men whose heads do grow beneath their shoulders." In his stories, Othello fashions himself into an adventurous and worldly man and it's this person that Desdemona fell in love with as she "devour[ed] up" Othello's stories with a "greedy ear."

We're also interested in what Othello's speech reveals about his new father-in-law, Brabantio. According to Othello, Brabantio "loved" him and "oft invited" Othello to tell stories about himself. It wasn't until Othello married Brabantio's daughter that the old man's xenophobia came to light.

My noble father,
I do perceive here a divided duty:
To you I am bound for life and education;
My life and education both do learn me
How to respect you; you are the lord of duty;
I am hitherto your daughter: but here's my husband,
And so much duty as my mother show'd
To you, preferring you before her father,
So much I challenge that I may profess
Due to the Moor my lord. (1.3.1)

Thought: Although Desdemona feels torn between her "duty" to her father and her husband
(kind of like Cordelia in Act 1 of *King Lear*), she ultimately professes her loyalty to her husband.
Here, we can see that Desdemona is tactful, respectful, and also pretty independent.

I saw Othello's visage in his mind,
And to his honour and his valiant parts
Did I my soul and fortunes consecrate.
So that, dear lords, if I be left behind,
A moth of peace, and he go to the war,
The rites for which I love him are bereft me,
And I a heavy interim shall support
By his dear absence. Let me go with him. (1.3.2)

Thought: There are a couple of things to notice about this passage. First, Desdemona says she
fell in love with the way Othello sees *himself*, which, as we know, is as a valiant war hero.
Second, we notice that Desdemona's pretty bold. She not only defends her right to marry the
man she loves but also her right to enjoy Othello as a husband, which includes being with him
when he leaves for Cyprus and sharing his bed. In other words, Desdemona's not afraid to
express her desire for her husband.

IAGO
Virtue! a fig! 'tis in ourselves that we are thus
or thus. Our bodies are our gardens, to the which
our wills are gardeners: so that if we will plant
nettles, or sow lettuce, set hyssop and weed up
thyme, supply it with one gender of herbs, or
distract it with many, either to have it sterile
with idleness, or manured with industry, why, the
power and corrigible authority of this lies in our
wills. If the balance of our lives had not one
scale of reason to poise another of sensuality, the
blood and baseness of our natures would conduct us
to most preposterous conclusions: but we have
reason to cool our raging motions, our carnal

stings, our unbitted lusts, whereof I take this that
you call love to be a sect or scion. (1.3.5)

Thought: Iago believes human beings have complete control over their actions and their emotions. Not only that, but Iago is also a figure who seems to have complete control over the actions and emotions of others, which we discuss in more detail in "Manipulation."

CASSIO
Reputation, reputation, reputation! O, I have lost
my reputation! I have lost the immortal part of
myself, and what remains is bestial. My reputation,
Iago, my reputation! (2.3.24)

Thought: After Cassio gets into a drunken brawl and loses his position as Othello's officer, he worries about the loss of his "reputation," which is tied up in his military service and his public behavior. Cassio feels that, without his "reputation" as an upstanding soldier, he's nothing more than a "beast."

for whiles this honest fool
Plies Desdemona to repair his fortunes
And she for him pleads strongly to the Moor,
I'll pour this pestilence into his ear,
That she repeals him for her body's lust;
And by how much she strives to do him good,
She shall undo her credit with the Moor.
So will I turn her virtue into pitch,
And out of her own goodness make the net
That shall enmesh them all. (2.3.31)

Thought: Earlier, we saw how Cassio sees his "reputation" as being the sum of his public behavior and his military service. Here, we can see that Desdemona's "reputation" hinges on her fidelity to her husband. When Iago says he's going to ruin Desdemona's "credit with the Moor," he means he's going to tarnish her reputation as a loyal wife ("turn her virtue into pitch").

OTHELLO
By heaven, I'll know thy thoughts.
IAGO
You cannot, if my heart were in your hand;
Nor shall not, whilst 'tis in my custody. (3.3.28)

Thought: Iago emphasizes that his real thoughts and feelings cannot be known by anyone—not Othello and not even the audience.

DESDEMONA
Alas, thrice-gentle Cassio!
My advocation is not now in tune;
My lord is not my lord; nor should I know him,
Were he in favour as in humour alter'd. (3.4.32)

IAGO
What's the matter, lady?
EMILIA
Alas, Iago, my lord hath so bewhored her.
Thrown such despite and heavy terms upon her,
As true hearts cannot bear.
DESDEMONA
Am I that name, Iago?
IAGO
What name, fair lady?
DESDEMONA
Such as she says my lord did say I was.
EMILIA
He call'd her whore: a beggar in his drink
Could not have laid such terms upon his callat.
IAGO
Why did he so?
DESDEMONA
I do not know; I am sure I am none such. (4.2.6)

Thought: At the play's beginning, Desdemona is strong, confident, and defiant but, after being victimized by Othello's physical and emotional abuse, she changes drastically. When Othello publicly abuses Desdemona, calling her a "whore" and even slapping her, Emilia is outraged. But Desdemona seems more confused and hurt than anything else. Here, Desdemona says she's "sure" that she's done absolutely nothing to warrant Othello's behavior and yet, we can detect a note of uncertainty. Soon after, Othello strangles her and Desdemona blames herself for her husband's violence. When Emilia asks Desdemona who has harmed her, Desdemona replies "Nobody; I myself. Farewell" (5.2.29).

LODOVICO
O thou Othello, thou wert once so good,
Fall'n in the practise of a damned slave,
What shall be said to thee?
OTHELLO
Why, any thing:
An honourable murderer, if you will;

For nought I did in hate, but all in honour. (5.2.3)

Thought: Yikes! Othello believes that murdering Desdemona was an "honourable" thing to do since he thought Desdemona was cheating on him. (Seems like Shakespeare is inviting us to disagree with Othello, wouldn't you say?) To the last, Othello wants to be identified as an honorable man but Lodovico asserts that Othello, the man who was "once so good" has "fall'n."

OTHELLO
Soft you; a word or two before you go.
I have done the state some service, and they know't.
No more of that. I pray you, in your letters,
When you shall these unlucky deeds relate,
Speak of me as I am; nothing extenuate,
Nor set down aught in malice: then must you speak
Of one that loved not wisely but too well;
Of one not easily jealous, but being wrought
Perplex'd in the extreme; of one whose hand,
Like the base Indian, threw a pearl away
Richer than all his tribe; of one whose subdued eyes,
Albeit unused to the melting mood,
Drop tears as fast as the Arabian trees
Their medicinal gum. Set you down this;
And say besides, that in Aleppo once,
Where a malignant and a turban'd Turk
Beat a Venetian and traduced the state,
I took by the throat the circumcised dog,
And smote him, thus. [kills himself][…]
(5.2.66)

Thought: Just before he commits suicide, Othello emphasizes his identity as a loyal soldier, which is how he wants to be remembered. At the same time, he also sees himself as a "malignant and a turban'd Turk" (a hated outsider and war opponent). By stabbing himself with the same sword he often used to kill enemy "Turks," Othello suggests that he sees himself as an enemy of the Venetian state.

IAGO
Demand me nothing: what you know, you know:
From this time forth I never will speak word. (5.2.11)

Thought: Iago refuses to explain himself. He conceals his motives and his true identity to the very last.

Plot Analysis

Classic Plot Analysis

Initial Situation

Wedding bells!

Othello and Desdemona fall in love and run away together to get married. Everything's peachy! Until Desdemona's father finds out…

Conflict

Interracial marriage not approved by Dad. Also, war and a villain.

The conflict comes in a few different forms. First, you've got Desdemona's dad all angry that his daughter secretly married a black man. Next, it looks like war with the Turks. Last and most importantly, you've got a livid Iago itching to wreak some havoc.

Complication

Iago hatches a plan.

While some of our conflicts go away (like the war and Brabantio, at least for the time being), others (Iago wanting to wreak havoc) lead to further complication. Iago is no longer an angry man; he's now an angry man with a plan. Not to mention, the convoluted machinations he devises are complicated enough in their own right, even without a classic plot analysis.

Climax

Iago convinces Othello that Desdemona's cheating and Othello resolves to kill her.

The intrigue of *Othello* is watching Iago work his manipulative magic. The deceptions grow, bit by bit, until Othello is quite ensnared by his own jealous thoughts. The plot thickens and thickens, and the complications twist and turn until we finally arrive at the psychological climax: Othello's declaration that he'll kill his wife. We chose this as the climax, rather than the actual killing, because we are building toward Iago's defeat of Othello's mind, not Othello's defeat of Desdemona's body.

Suspense

Othello will soon kill Desdemona.

Now that we know Othello's going to kill Desdemona, we get all worked up in the suspense of when it's actually going to happen. We're also not sure how things will work out for Iago. Will he get away with his plan?

Denouement

Almost everybody dies.

The denouement starts as soon as Desdemona dies. Minutes after she dies, Emilia figures out that Iago is responsible for the whole mess. When she shares this with Othello and his men, Iago kills her. Othello, broken by grief and guilt, stabs himself.

Conclusion

Bizarre silence from Iago.
Cassio survives. So does Iago, who refuses to explain why he did what he did and swears he will never speak again. It's an unsatisfying conclusion, since we wanted the cash-in moment where the detective explains who did what in what room with whom.

Booker's Seven Basic Plots Analysis: Five-Part Tragedy

Anticipation Stage
Desdemona and Othello get married and look forward to a happy life together.
War interrupts their romance, but they assume they'll have time together soon.

Dream Stage
Welcome to Cyprus, Island of Love
Everything is wonderful with Desdemona and Othello. The newlyweds have each other, they're surrounded by trusted friends (or so they think), there's no war…

Frustration Stage
Evil Iago convinces Othello that Desdemona is cheating on him. At first, Othello can't believe it, but Iago gradually warps his mind.
Needless to say, it is rather frustrating for a newly married man to be told his wife is already screwing around. This is definitely your teeth-gritting stage.

Nightmare Stage
Othello begins to go almost crazy with jealousy. His love for Desdemona is changed to disgust. He mistreats her, even hitting her in public, and calls her a whore. Desdemona can't understand what's happening to the man she loves.
Teeth-gritting proceeds duly to jaw-dropping, as Iago's machinations increase in complexity and general evilness. Othello's suspicions stop being suspicions and become, in his mind, undeniable truths. The psychological heart of this stage is when Othello commits to killing Desdemona. The physical peak is when he hits her, in public.

Destruction
Othello kills Desdemona and plans on Iago killing Cassio; Iago convinces Roderigo to kill Cassio but ends up wounding Cassio himself and killing Roderigo; Othello finds out the truth and kills himself, but not before trying to kill Iago, who also kills Emilia.
Keep in mind that this is the destruction not only of everyone's life, but also of the dream that we started with way back in the early part of the story.

Study Questions

1. In what way is *Othello*'s race relevant to the events of the play?
2. Compare and contrast Desdemona and Emilia's views on love, sex, marriage, and men.

Do either Desdemona or Emilia change their viewpoints as a result of their conversations with each other?

3. Why does Iago want to destroy Othello?

4. Iago is constantly talking about women in derogatory ways, from his joking assessment of women for the amusement of Desdemona in the second act to his put-downs of Emilia to his assumption that Desdemona will probably cheat on Othello eventually. Does the play support Iago's opinion of women, or refute it?

5. Check out Iago and Desdemona's views on love and sex. Are they similar? Different? Does Iago believe in love at all? What relationship might Desdemona draw between love and sex? Does the play ultimately endorse either of their views?

6. In what ways are the marriages of Desdemona/Othello and Emilia/Iago similar? In what ways are they different?

7. Who is a more jealous person, Othello or Iago?

8. Who does Othello ultimately care about more – Desdemona or himself? Some critics have argued that Othello's love of Desdemona is ultimately self-centered. Would you agree? Does this mean that, without Iago, they would have lived happily ever after?

9. "She loved me for the dangers I had passed, / And I loved her that she did pity them" (1.3.167-168). This is how Othello describes how he and Desdemona fell for each other. What does this tell you about their relationship? Check out the lines 1.3.128-170 carefully. How do you envision their interactions? What kind of relationship is portrayed in this passage?

10. In *Othello*, most of the action takes place between only two characters: Iago and Othello, and this "action" is basically intense conversation and plotting. What effect does this produce on us as a reader? What challenges does this pose for directors and actors? Is *Othello* a domestic drama? Does it feel claustrophobic? How does the scale and focus of the play reflect the themes of jealousy, hatred and obsession?

11. In 1998, Patrick Stewart, a white actor, played the role of Othello surrounded by an all-black cast. Do you think this way of performing *Othello* would be effective? Would it substantially change any of the themes or dynamics of the play? Which ones?

12. There are only three women in the play: Desdemona, Emilia (both wives), and Bianca (a prostitute in love with one of her clients). What insight does the play provide into women's lives? How does the addition of Bianca, a prostitute, to the play emphasize or contradict different characters' ways of thinking about women? Compare and contrast Bianca's relationship to Cassio with Desdemona and Emilia's relationships with their husbands.

13. Desdemona's love for Othello is unconditional. Even when he hits her and calls her a whore, she still says she loves him. At the end, she says she killed herself rather than tell the truth and implicate Othello. Is Desdemona's overwhelming love admirable? Should we pity Desdemona rather than admiring her? What would your advice to Desdemona be?

14. The plot of the play hinges on the loss of a handkerchief Othello gave to Desdemona. Two little deceptions – Emilia's stealing of the handkerchief and Desdemona's lie to Othello that it is not lost – cement Desdemona's doom. What does it mean that such a little object has such a huge impact on Othello's mind? What dramatic effect does this produce? Do you think that, in a situation of jealousy, even a handkerchief could sway someone's opinion one way or another? Is the importance of the handkerchief in the play believable?

Characters

All Characters

Othello Character Analysis

Othello is the first great black protagonist in Western literature, and still one of the most famous. The play dramatizes this hero's fall from grace – Othello begins as a noble guy (he's a celebrated and respected war hero, a loving husband, and an eloquent storyteller) but, by the end of the play, Othello has become an irrational, violent, and insanely jealous husband who murders his own wife after Iago convinces him that Desdemona has been unfaithful.

Othello's Status in Venice
A black man from North Africa, Othello has traveled the world, been sold into slavery, escaped, and ended up as the military commander of the Venetian military, guard to a powerful Italian city-state. Othello's status in Venice is pretty complicated – he's both an insider and an outsider. On the one hand, he is a Christian and experienced military leader, commanding respect and admiration from the Duke, the Senate, and many Venetian citizens. On the other hand, being a black Moor and a foreigner in Venice also subjects Othello to some overt racism, especially by his wife's father, who believes Desdemona's interracial marriage can only be the result of Othello's trickery (1.2.1).

Fears of Miscegenation
According to Brabantio, Othello must have "enchanted" Desdemona with "foul charms" and magic spells. Otherwise, he insists, Desdemona never would never have run "to the sooty bosom" of Othello (1.2.2). In the play, Othello's marriage to Desdemona prompts some characters to refer to Othello as "thick-lips," the "devil," and the "old black ram" that supposedly contaminates a white woman (Desdemona) with his hyper-sexuality. At one point, Iago suggests that Othello is a "devil" that will make Brabantio the "grandsire" of black (like the devil) babies (1.1.10).

Many literary critics have pointed out that the play seems to capture some pretty common (and pretty awful) sixteenth and seventeenth attitudes toward interracial couplings. We can also draw some parallels between the play and more contemporary attitudes in the U.S. Here's what actor Paul Robeson (the black American actor who broke the color barrier when he played Othello on Broadway in 1943) had to say about Othello:

"In the Venice of that time [Othello] was in practically the same position as a coloured man in America today [1930]. He was a general, and while he could be valuable as a fighter he was tolerated, just as a negro who could save New York from a disaster would become a great man overnight. So soon, however, as Othello wanted a white woman, Desdemona, everything was changed, just as New York would be indignant if their coloured man married a white woman." (See "My Fight for Fame. How Shakespeare Paved My Way to Stardom." *Pearson's Weekly*, April 5, 1930, p 100.)

The 1930s may seem like a very long time ago, but it would be a mistake to say that Shakespeare's work and Paul Robeson's remarks are not relevant today. As recently as October 2009, a white Justice of the Peace in Louisiana refused to marry an interracial couple (source).

Othello's Suspicion

Despite the taboo of an interracial marriage, Othello and Desdemona are pretty happy and in love at the beginning of the play. So, what the heck happens? Why does Othello become convinced that his faithful wife is cheating on him? We know that Iago manipulates Othello with his lies about Desdemona, but Iago never actually offers up any real proof of Desdemona's "affair," which suggests that Othello is pretty gullible.

There are a couple of ways we can read Othello's eagerness to believe the worst about his wife. Some literary critics suggest that Othello believes that *all* women are inherently promiscuous. This seems to be the case when he says things like all men are "destined" to be cuckolded by their wives (3.3.42). Other critics argue that Othello begins to absorb the racist attitudes that surround him in Venice. In other words, Othello begins to believe that 1) he's not good enough for Desdemona because he's black and 2) as a black man, his relationship with his wife may "soil" her, which we discuss in more detail in our discussion the theme of "Race."

Self-Absorbed Othello?

We may also want to consider another possibility. The one Othello loves "too well" isn't Desdemona – it's himself. Jealousy is an intensely self-centered emotion, and Othello spends much of the play obsessed with how Desdemona has hurt him and trying to get back at her for it. He's obsessed with *his* feelings, the way that her cheating reflects on *him*.

Scholar Marjorie Garber suggests that Othello's self-absorption starts way before Iago gets to him. She points out that Othello equates his inner, personal life with his outer, professional life. He can't draw any boundaries between them. Most people may not believe, as Othello does, that a problem in their personal life could destroy their ability to function in their careers. But in Othello's scene with the Senate, he's eager to assure the senators that he won't let his marriage get in the way of his career. And when Othello thinks Desdemona has cheated on him, his first reaction is to declare, "Farewell the pluméd troops and the big wars… Othello's occupation's gone" (3.3.49).

Othello's destructiveness, his determination to punish Desdemona for cheating on him, stems from his rage that Desdemona's immoral actions have also damaged him. What makes Othello so furious, Garber suggests, is that, when it comes to himself, Othello is a perfectionist. This all reflects rather poorly on Othello.

But let's take a step back. Why is Othello a self-obsessed perfectionist in the first place? Othello's dangerous perfectionism may stem from his position as an outsider, a black man in white Venetian society. Othello only could have risen to his position of power through incredible self-discipline. To be fair to Othello, we have to consider carefully *why* he is so obsessed with his own self-image, and why he is so easily persuaded that Desdemona would tire of him and move on to another man. To the extent that these factors are the result of Othello's outsider

status and the prejudice he constantly has to overcome, we may want to cut Othello some slack.

Othello Timeline and Summary

- 1.1 Iago reveals that Othello has secretly married Desdemona.
- 1.2 Othello faces a showdown with Brabantio, Desdemona's angry father. The tiff is cut short when the Duke orders that Othello get himself over to the Duke's chambers, sooner rather than later.
- 1.3 Othello explains how Desdemona and he fell in love. Desdemona has his back. The Duke says the marriage seems legit, and sends Othello off to fight an enemy fleet.
- 2.1 The enemy fleet destroyed, Othello arrives at Cyprus and joyfully greets his wife. It's time for the honeymoon.
- 2.3 Othello and Desdemona finally get some alone time, but then they're interrupted when Cassio gets into a drunken brawl. Othello, furious, fires him.
- 3.2 Othello and Iago tour the city.
- 3.3 Othello comes back to find Cassio slinking away from a conversation with Desdemona. He and his wife play-fight in that annoying newlywed way. But Iago slowly starts messing with Othello's mind and convinces Othello that Desdemona's cheating on him with Cassio. Othello demands proof of Iago's claim, but already believes him, proof or not. He swears to punish his wife and Cassio with death.
- 3.4 Othello, suspicious, asks Desdemona where the special handkerchief he gave her is. Because Iago has had it stolen, Desdemona can't produce it. She doesn't want to admit this, though, so she and Othello get in a huge fight.
- 4.1 Iago torments Othello with more graphic images of Desdemona's cheating, so much so that Othello has a brief epileptic fit. Then Iago sets up a conversation with Cassio so that Othello thinks he's hearing them talk about Desdemona when, really, Cassio's talking about a prostitute. After this, when Desdemona comes in with a visitor announcing that Othello is called back to Venice, Othello gets so angry that he hits his wife in front of everyone.
- 4.2 Othello tries to get Emilia to confess that Desdemona is having an affair. Emilia says it just isn't true. Then Othello confronts Desdemona and calls her a whore. Desdemona denies it, but Othello doesn't believe her.
- 5.1 Othello oversees what he thinks is Cassio's murder, and is satisfied.
- 5.2 Othello strangles Desdemona. Emilia comes in and raises the alarm. When Othello tells her why he thinks Desdemona cheated on him, Emilia realizes that this must be a plot by her husband. She tells Othello the truth, and he responds by trying to stab Iago and failing in the process. Iago refuses to tell Othello why he destroyed his life. Othello, heartbroken, stabs himself and dies next to Desdemona.

Iago Character Analysis

Iago is one of the most notorious and mysterious villains of all time. He spends all of his time plotting against Othello and Desdemona, eventually convincing Othello that his wife has been cheating, despite the fact that Desdemona has been completely faithful. Iago's capacity for cruelty seems limitless, and no motivation he gives for his actions seems enough to explain the incredible destruction he wreaks on the lives of the people he knows best.

Iago as a Masterful Plotter

Shakespeare scholar Harold Bloom argues that Iago is an artist of evil. The same way that some people enjoy writing songs or filming movies, Iago enjoys ruining people's lives. He does it with a sense of craftsmanship, appreciating the elegance or cleverness of a particular step in his scheme as much as its final result: incredible suffering for the people he has chosen. Ever notice how he stops every time he does something cleverly evil, to muse on it and tell us how awesome he is? Exactly.

We tend to think of evil people as being brutal and insensitive, or at least disconnected from the people they hurt. Iago, however, is able to hurt Othello so much because he understands him so well. He even grows closer to Othello as his plot progresses. Iago manipulates him so expertly that at times it seems he is actually inside Othello's head.

Iago's Motives

Most other Shakespearean characters do bad things in order to achieve a particular goal. Oftentimes the culprit is ambition, as in *Macbeth*, or revenge, as in *Hamlet*. The thing about Iago is this – we never really know for certain *why* it is that Iago wants to destroy Othello. Throughout the play, Iago provides multiple and incompatible motives for hating Othello. At one point, Iago says he's angry because Othello passed him over for a promotion. Later, he claims to suspect that Othello is having an affair with his (Iago's) wife (Emilia).

So, what are we to make of this? On the one hand, we could say that Iago has no real motives – he's just plain evil. Poet Samuel Taylor Coleridge calls Iago "a being next to the devil, only not quite the devil" and goes on to call Iago's behavior "motiveless malignity." If we agree that Iago has no *real* motives for hurting Othello, we could also argue that Iago's character is kind of "Vice" figure. A "Vice" figure is stock character from medieval Morality plays like "Everyman." Vice figures are typically personifications of, well, vice (immoral behavior) – they tend to be tempters and often agents of the devil. (By the way, Richard II, of Shakespeare's play, *Richard II*, is also often seen as a kind of Vice figure.) Iago is a lot more complex than most Vice figures but we can definitely see how Shakespeare is borrowing from literary tradition.

Is Iago in Lust with Othello?

What? You don't like the "motiveless malignancy" theory? Fine. Here's another explanation that some critics like. Iago secretly wants to get it on with Othello and ends up hurting Othello because he's jealous of Desdemona. (Orson Welles seemed partial to this idea – his film version of the drama exploits the homoerotic undertones of the play and Iago basically woos Othello away from Desdemona.) If you think this idea may be worth exploring (or if you just want to know what the heck Orson Welles was thinking), be sure to check out Act 3, Scene 4, line 64,

the passage where Othello makes Iago his new lieutenant and Iago vows to kill Cassio. It sounds a whole lot like a sixteenth-century wedding ceremony, which suggests a homoerotic attachment between Iago and Othello.

No matter how you choose to interpret it, think about the fact that Iago is often our focus in this play. We follow his storyline more than Othello's and we spend more time with him than Othello. We watch him in a variety of relationships – his manipulation of Roderigo, his treatment of his wife, his pseudo-friendship with Othello. If it weren't for the fact that Iago undergoes basically no changes, you could even argue that he's the main character.

Iago Timeline and Summary

- 1.1 Iago tells Roderigo about Othello's marriage. Together they rat out Othello and Desdemona to Desdemona's father.
- 1.2 Iago warns Othello that Desdemona's father is coming.
- 1.3 After the Duke approves the marriage, Roderigo wants to give up and drown himself. Iago convinces him that he can still get Desdemona in the end. Iago decides to convince Othello that Desdemona's cheating on him.
- 2.1 Iago arrives at Cyprus with Desdemona and his own wife, Emilia. To amuse Desdemona, Iago says lots of nasty, clever things about women. Later, Iago convinces Roderigo that Cassio and Desdemona are getting it on, and decides that he will use Cassio to make Othello jealous. He convinces Roderigo to fight with Cassio in order to get Cassio in trouble.
- 2.3 Iago gets Cassio drunk, watches him get into a brawl, and then tells Othello all about it. After Cassio is fired, Iago suggests to him that he ask Desdemona to intervene with Othello in his favor. Cassio thinks this is a great idea. Iago gloats about how well his plan is working.
- 3.1 Iago makes sure his wife will bring Cassio in to talk with Desdemona.
- 3.2 Iago and Othello tour the city.
- 3.3 Iago begins with small comments and gradually reels Othello in until he tells him point blank that Desdemona is cheating on him. Othello demands proof and Iago promises to give him some. Then Iago swears that he will help Othello revenge himself on Desdemona.
- 3.4 Iago comes in with Cassio and finds Desdemona upset at Othello's weird behavior. He promises her he will find out what's wrong.
- 4.1 Iago stages a conversation with Cassio such that Othello, overhearing, thinks they're talking about Desdemona. In fact, they're talking about a prostitute (Bianca) who is in love with Cassio.
- 4.2 Iago convinces Roderigo that he should kill Cassio.
- 5.1 Iago watches Roderigo try to kill Cassio. Then Iago stabs Cassio from behind. When more of Othello's soldiers appear, Iago stabs Roderigo too, as if trying to help Cassio. Then Iago tries to pin all the blame on Bianca, Cassio's prostitute lover.
- 5.2 After Othello strangles Desdemona, Emilia starts to realize what Iago has done. He tells her to shut up, but she tells Othello and everyone present that Iago is to blame for the whole situation. Othello tries to stab him, but instead Iago stabs Emilia and runs out. He's

captured and brought back in, but he refuses to explain why he did all these terrible things. He swears he will never speak again.

Desdemona Character Analysis

Desdemona is a beautiful, young, white, Venetian debutante, her father's pride and joy. But she refuses to marry any of the rich, handsome Venetian men that everyone expects her to marry. Instead, she elopes with Othello – an older black man, an outsider to Venetian society. Turns out, this is a pretty gutsy move – Desdemona not only defies her father's expectations (that she marry a white man of his choosing), she also thumbs her nose at a society that largely disapproves of interracial marriages. In this way, Desdemona's relationship with Othello speaks to the play's concerns with sixteenth century attitudes about sex, gender, and race, which we discuss in more detail in our "Themes" section.

From "Fair Warrior" to Victim of Abuse

Like Othello, Desdemona undergoes a dramatic transformation over the course of the play. At the play's beginning, Desdemona's an adventurous spirit – when her new husband is called away for military duty in Cyprus, she begs to go with him and can't stand the thought of remaining at home, where there isn't any action. This isn't so surprising, given that Desdemona seems to be drawn to Othello's exciting past. We learn that Othello wooed Desdemona by telling stories of action, adventure, and danger, and that Desdemona consumed these tales with a "greedy ear." We also know that Desdemona has said she wishes "the heavens had made her a man like Othello," which could mean that she wanted to *marry* a man like Othello, or that wishes she *were a man* like Othello, instead of a woman (1.3.4).

Desdemona's also pretty frank about her sexual desire for her husband, which is part of the reason why she wants to go with him to Cyprus. At times, Desdemona also seems a bit naïve, especially when it comes to marital relationships – at one point, she asks an incredulous Emilia if it's possible that a woman would ever cheat on her husband. This gives us a hint as to why Desdemona doesn't seem to have a clue that Othello suspects her of infidelity – for Desdemona, the idea is simply unthinkable. Despite her loyalty to her husband, Othello physically and verbally abuses Desdemona, slapping her and calling her a whore in public. By the play's end, Desdemona is so beaten down that she's rather passive when Othello strangles her and when, with her dying breath, she blames herself for Othello's physical and emotional abuse. This is a stark reminder that Desdemona is the real victim in this tragic play.

Do Othello and Desdemona Ever Consummate Their Marriage?

Shakespeare scholar Harold Bloom thinks that Desdemona's virginity is the big driving question of the play. Bloom argues that Othello and Desdemona never had sex – that Desdemona actually dies a virgin. He points out that every time the newlyweds come close, something interrupts them – an order to come see the Duke, a war, or Cassio's drunken brawl. When Desdemona and Othello first arrive in Cyprus, it's clear they haven't had sex yet. After all, Othello says it explicitly. What happens next – whether Cassio's fight really prevents any sex at all that night – is less clear. But Bloom argues that what makes Othello's jealousy so tortuous is

that the only way he can figure out if Desdemona is actually cheating with him or not is to have sex with her. If she's still a virgin, she's been faithful. But, Bloom suggests, Othello just can't take the pressure of sleeping with his wife and realizing in the act that she's not a virgin, which would prove that she must have been sleeping around.

Other literary scholars argue that Othello and Desdemona *do* eventually consummate their marriage in the play, just before their lovemaking is interrupted by Cassio's drunken brawl. This is the reason why Othello goes nuts – according to this theory, Othello believes that his black skin color makes him contaminat*ed* and contaminat*ing*. When he has sex with Desdemona, Othello thinks he's polluted her pure, white body, and he just can't stand it. As we know, several characters (like Brabantio and Iago) claim that black men like Othello contaminate white women they have sexual contact with. If it's true that Othello believes he's polluted Desdemona and turned her into a filthy "whore," then it would mean that Othello has internalized the racism that he encounters in the play.

Desdemona Timeline and Summary

- 1.1 Iago reveals that Desdemona has secretly married Othello.
- 1.2 Desdemona tells her father and the Duke that she married Othello out of love. Then she asks permission to travel with him when he goes to war in Cyprus.
- 2.1 Desdemona gets to Cyprus first and worries about Othello until he gets there.
- 2.3 The happy couple is interrupted when Othello has to settle a fight. Desdemona joins, upset, and asks her husband what's going on.
- 3.3 Cassio asks Desdemona to help him get his job back after Othello fired him for fighting drunkenly the night before. Desdemona agrees to sweet talk Othello until he gives in and says he'll take Cassio back. Later, Desdemona comes in and finds Othello upset. She tries to comfort him, but accidentally drops the special handkerchief that Othello gave her.
- 3.4 Othello demands to see the handkerchief. Desdemona doesn't have it, but she lies and says it isn't lost. She tries to have him promise to give Cassio his job back. Othello and Desdemona have their first big fight, and she's still shell-shocked when Cassio and Iago come in. But she gradually convinces herself that she's wrong to blame Othello for the fight – she can't expect him to be sweet all the time, and fighting is normal.
- 4.1 Othello slaps Desdemona in public.
- 4.2 Othello confronts Desdemona and tries to make her confess she's a whore. She denies it, but he doesn't believe her. Desdemona begs Iago to help her figure out what's wrong with her husband.
- 4.3 Getting ready for bed, Desdemona broods over Othello's strange behavior. She starts singing a depressing song about a woman whose lover deserts her. Then she asks Emilia if there really are women who cheat on their husbands. Desdemona can't believe anyone would do that.
- 5.2 Desdemona wakes up to find Othello hanging out over her with a creepy look on his face. It doesn't take long for her to realize that he's going to kill her. She tries to convince him that she's innocent, and then begs him to delay her death for even a few minutes. He refuses and smothers her. But she's not quite dead – yet. When Emilia enters,

Desdemona utters with her final breaths that she is innocent, but still refuses to pin the blame for her death on Othello.

Emilia Character Analysis

Older and more cynical than Desdemona, Emilia develops a close relationship with the young married woman. Emilia and Desdemona bond over husband trouble: Emilia's bitter take on her married life with Iago contrasts with Desdemona's (temporarily) idealistic marriage to Othello.

Emilia's one dishonest act towards Desdemona – stealing her special handkerchief – turns out to have devastating consequences. The loss of the handkerchief is what convinces Othello that Desdemona is guilty of infidelity, and Emilia's little theft ends up causing her friend's death, at least in part.

But she redeems herself, or it least gives a good shot at trying. It is Emilia who discovers the truth about Iago's plotting and reveals it to the world. She can't bring Desdemona back to life, but she does clear her friend's name. She ends up sacrificing her life so that Desdemona won't be remembered as a "whore." Iago kills Emilia as payback for unmasking him, but Emilia dies proud that she set the record straight.

Emilia's relationship with Iago really seems like a marriage made in hell. Iago constantly mocks and disrespects her. He never seems to offer her any affection, and he always talks trash about women in general. Despite this, Emilia seems eager to please him. She steals Desdemona's handkerchief in the hope that Iago will appreciate her for once. "I nothing but to please his fantasy," she says as she does so (3.3). But her attempt to make the handkerchief hand-off a teasing, flirtatious interaction fails miserably. Iago grabs the handkerchief and tells her to go away. Later, it seems like Emilia is aware of Iago's thirst for power and wishes she could gratify it. She asks Desdemona, "Who would not make her husband a cuckold to make him a monarch? I should venture purgatory for't" (4.3).

So Emilia ends up looking like that poor girl with no self-confidence who's with that awful guy because she craves affection. Emilia goes so far as to betray her friend for the love of her man. And yet, despite her submissiveness, Emilia's obvious bitterness boils over in a final scene during which she says that husbands are usually to blame when their wives cheat on them. After all, men cheat on women all the time – why shouldn't women have an equal right to infidelity? Considering that this was written in the early 1600s, Emilia's monologue is about as close as we will get to a feminist manifesto. But like Shylock's "Hath not a Jew eyes" speech in Shakespeare's _Merchant of Venice_, it's not the best argument for equality. Shylock argues that Jews are people, too – and so they have an equal right to revenge. Emilia argues that women are people, too – and so they should have an equal right to cheat on their spouses. These aren't the most uplifting messages.

Throughout most of the play, Iago has the upper hand in his interactions with his wife. But the final scene is payback time for Emilia. Shakespeare scholar Harold Bloom points out that of all

the people in the play, Emilia is the only one that Iago underestimates – and she's the only one who ultimately can bring Iago down. That's an interesting irony. Iago, who is so good at predicting and manipulating other people's behavior, only fails to understand one person – the person he should have known best.

Emilia Timeline and Summary

- 2.1 Emilia comes to Cyprus with Desdemona and her husband, Iago, who constantly mocks her.
- 3.1 Cassio asks Emilia if she can bring him to talk to Desdemona. Emilia agrees.
- 3.3 Emilia steals Desdemona's handkerchief and gives it to her husband. He isn't particularly grateful.
- 3.4 Desdemona searches for the lost handkerchief; Emilia says nothing. When Desdemona and Othello fight, Emilia suggests that he's acting jealous.
- 4.2 Othello interrogates Emilia about whether Desdemona is having an affair with Cassio. Emilia insists Desdemona is innocent. After Othello has another fight with his wife, during which he calls her a whore, Emilia tries to comfort Desdemona. She says Othello is acting just as crazy as Iago did when Iago thought that she and Othello were having an affair. Iago tells her to shut up.
- 4.3 Emilia helps Desdemona prepare for bed. Desdemona asks her if she thinks women really do cheat on their husbands. Emilia says she would cheat on her husband if the payoff were big enough. Then she rants about the double standard between men's behavior and women's behavior.
- 5.1 Emilia comes upon the chaos surrounding Cassio and his being wounded in a mysterious attack. Iago sends her to tell the news to Othello.
- 5.2 Emilia comes into Desdemona's bedroom to find Othello there and Desdemona lying near death. Desdemona says she has been falsely murdered, then dies. Othello admits to doing it and says Desdemona deserved it. Emilia, not caring if Othello kills her, screams and raises the alarm. As Othello keeps talking about the handkerchief, Emilia realizes that Iago must be at fault for Othello's misinformation. She accuses her husband in front of Othello and other witnesses. Othello realizes the truth, and Iago stabs Emilia in revenge. She dies next to Desdemona, pleased with herself for having spoken the truth.

Michael Cassio Character Analysis

When we begin, Cassio is one of Othello's soldiers, and is recently appointed the general's second-in-command. This infuriates Iago, as he wanted to be lieutenant, and Cassio is a math (not muscle) guy, so Iago cannot understand this appointment.

Like all people, real and imagined, he's got some flaws. First, he's a lightweight when it comes to drinking. This is the weakness that Iago exploits (when Iago gets Cassio drunk and sends him off to fight Roderigo). Second, Cassio's a little too much of a lady's man. This angers Iago,

as Cassio's kissing Emilia in front of Iago is a bad idea. It also comes back to bite Cassio in the end, since his flirtatious charisma helps convince Othello that Cassio is having sex with Desdemona.

Cassio is the kind of guy who likes to put women in one of two categories – virgin or whore. When he talks about Desdemona, we can tell that he sees her as a kind of secular Virgin Mary. Here's what he says when Desdemona arrives in Cyprus:

O behold [...] You men of Cyprus, let her have your knees,
Hail to thee lady! And the grace of heaven,
Before, behind thee, and on every hand,
Enwheel thee round. (2.1.8)

Clearly, Cassio worships Desdemona but, he has a tendency to mock his courtesan girlfriend, Bianca, who, sadly, is pretty smitten with Cassio. As Iago points out, "when [Cassio] hears of [Bianca], he cannot refrain / From the excess of laughter" (4.1.19). While Cassio may not be guilty of sleeping with another man's wife, it seems pretty clear that he's kind of a jerk when it comes to women.

Michael Cassio Timeline and Summary

- 1.1 Iago announces that Othello has recently chosen Cassio for his second-in-command.
- 1.2 Cassio shows up with a message to Othello from the Duke: get over here.
- 2.1 Cassio is there to greet Desdemona, Othello, and Iago when they arrive at Cyprus. He is very friendly to them both and kisses Emilia hello, which does not please Iago.
- 2.3 After Iago gets him drunk, Cassio fights with Roderigo, and then with Montano, who's just trying to calm him down. Othello comes out, furious at the disorder, and fires Cassio. Iago suggests that Cassio turn to Desdemona to convince Othello to re-hire him.
- 3.1 Iago goes to Emilia and asks to be taken to Desdemona. She agrees.
- 3.3 Desdemona agrees to help Cassio get his job back. He's grateful, but slinks away when he sees Othello coming back.
- 3.4 Cassio comes in to see if Desdemona has succeeded in getting him his job back, but Desdemona and Othello have just had a fight, so it's not a good time. Later, Cassio gives Bianca (a prostitute he's involved with) a handkerchief he found in his room. Apparently he liked the pattern on it so much that he wanted Bianca to copy it. It happens to belong to Desdemona, stolen by Emilia on behalf of the scheming Iago. Trouble is a-brewing.
- 4.1 Cassio comes in and sees Othello in the middle of a fit. Iago assures him it's a normal thing and asks to talk to him later. Cassio comes back and jokes with Iago about Bianca and how needy and ridiculous she is. (Othello, overhearing, thinks they're discussing Desdemona.) Then Bianca comes in and throws the handkerchief back in Cassio's face; she's sure it's from some other woman, and who does he think he is!? Unfortunately, Othello is watching.
- 5.1 Cassio's minding his own business when Roderigo tries to attack him. Cassio beats him off, but Iago secretly wounds him from behind. Cassio falls and shouts for help.

- 5.2 Cassio, not dead, comes in after Othello has killed Desdemona to confirm that she never had an affair with him and that this was all Iago's terrible plot against them. While Othello has to go back to Venice to get punished for killing his wife, Cassio gets to take his (military) position in Cyprus.

Roderigo Character Analysis

Roderigo is a rich, unintelligent guy who thinks that if he sends Desdemona enough expensive presents, she'll fall in love with him. He's hired Iago to be his wingman, but Iago basically uses him as a walking ATM. Iago takes the jewelry Roderigo thinks he's giving to Desdemona and sells it for a profit. All Roderigo does in response is to fall for Iago's smooth talking again and again. In the end, Roderigo dies – stabbed in the back, appropriately enough, by his wingman, Iago.

Roderigo Timeline and Summary

- 1.1 Roderigo freaks out when he realizes that Desdemona is marrying Othello instead of him. He blames Iago for not realizing this earlier. Iago tells him it's not over yet; they wake up Desdemona's father and tell him he'd better find his runaway daughter.
- 1.2 When the Duke approves of Othello and Desdemona's marriage, Roderigo says he'd better give up and drown himself. Iago convinces him to get more money, under the pretense that he can seduce Desdemona much more easily once she's Othello's desperate housewife.
- 2.1 Iago convinces Roderigo that Desdemona is already getting it on with Cassio, and that he has to beat Cassio up since he's the competition.
- 2.3 Roderigo gets in a fight with drunken Cassio, but only manages to get beat up himself. He talks about giving up and going back to Venice, but Iago persuades him to keep trying.
- 4.2 Roderigo finally shows some spine. He accuses Iago of not being up front with him, and he's suspicious that Desdemona has not received all the jewels he sent her. He threatens to make Iago pay if he doesn't produce results ASAP. Iago, however, just praises Roderigo for his boldness and tells him he needs to kill Cassio if he wants to take the place in Desdemona's bed. Once again, Roderigo is persuaded.
- 5.1 Roderigo tries to kill Cassio and fails, so Iago stabs and kills Roderigo. This way, he won't be able to betray their scheming. Iago is a "I don't want any loose ends" kind of guy.

Brabantio Character Analysis

Desdemona's father, Brabantio, is a rich and important Venetian politician. He likes Othello and invites him to visit his house a lot — but he never expected Othello "to steal" his daughter.

Further, he never believed his little girl would marry Othello unless she was drugged or under some kind of spell.

Like many Shakespearean fathers (think Baptista Minola from *The Taming of the Shrew* or Portia's dad, who arranges his daughter's marriage from his grave in *The Merchant of Venice*), Brabantio tends to see his daughter as his property, which means that he sees marriage as a potential business transaction. Brabantio's irrational fears about his daughter's interracial marriage make him a central figure in the play's examination of race and sex, which you can read more about in our "Themes" section. Brabantio apparently dies of grief after his daughter runs off with Othello.

Bianca Character Analysis

Bianca is a Venetian courtesan who is in love with Cassio, who sees her as a laughable nuisance. Shakespeare's portrayal of Bianca is sympathetic – when Cassio treats her like garbage, it's clear that Shakespeare's making a point about how women get used throughout the play.

We know what you're wondering. Why would Shakespeare go out of his way to make one of just three female characters in the play a *prostitute*? Here's what we think is going on. Because Bianca is a courtesan in a city renowned for prostitution and promiscuity, she's a foil to the chaste and ever-faithful Desdemona. Othello, however, doesn't recognize the difference between these women – he's persuaded that Desdemona is cheating even though there's no real proof. This speaks to a much larger issue in the play, which is that all three women are accused at some point or another of being promiscuous, which we talk about more in "Gender."

Duke, Senators Character Analysis

The important men in charge of Venice. They think Othello's pretty great – even that he might make a pretty great son-in-law.

Lodovico Character Analysis

Desdemona's cousin and a member of Venice's diplomatic service, Lodovico arrives in Cyprus just in time to see Desdemona get slapped by her new husband, and then witness the deaths of all the main characters, and the twisted revelations of jealousy and betrayal. He has no personality – he's just a witness. But, like Horatio in *Hamlet*, Lodovico is the guy who survives the inevitable bloodbath at the play's end and promises to tell the world about the tragedy that has just unfolded.

Montano Character Analysis

Governor of Cyprus before Othello showed up to take command, Montano ends up getting in a fight with Cassio, and in turn gets Cassio in serious trouble.

Gratiano Character Analysis

Desdemona's uncle – when he finds out that Desdemona is dead, he says something lame like "Gee, it's a good thing her dad is dead, otherwise he would have been really upset by all this."

Character Roles

Protagonist
Othello
Othello is the tragic protagonist of the story. The play revolves around Othello's corruption by Iago and his descent into a dangerous jealousy. What's interesting is that we spend more time with the villain than the protagonist, one of the more unique qualities of *Othello*. But even though he spends a bit of time off-stage, the plot is still centered on Othello, and more importantly, the destruction of Othello.

Antagonist
Iago
You can't get much more antagonistic than Iago is towards Othello. At the same time, you could make the argument that Iago is the real protagonist, since his character dominates the play and he is the one with the most soliloquies (which is a pretty clear "main character" signal in most Shakespeare plays). But, Iago doesn't really change at all and, as we know, most protagonists undergo some kind of change over the course of a play.

The roles of protagonist and antagonist are more intimately bound together in *Othello* than in most of Shakespeare's plays. From the opening lines, Iago describes himself not just as Othello's antagonist, but also as a person who wants to completely destroy Othello's life. Iago stays close to Othello so he can rip apart everything that Othello cares about almost from the inside out. Iago understands Othello so well that at some points it seems like he has become a voice inside Othello's head, constantly tormenting him with new doubts.

Foil
Emilia to Desdemona
An older, more experienced, more cynical woman, Emilia's attitude towards men contrasts with Desdemona's naïve idealism. Think, for example, of Desdemona's naïveté when she wonders if there are any women that would actually cheat on their husbands. Emilia's response is more worldly – she says something like, "Yep, there sure are women who cheat on their husbands." Not only that, Emilia says "[b]ut I do think it is their husbands' faults / If wives do fall" (4.3.16). Check out our discussion for "Gender" for more on this.

Character Clues

Actions

Actions are interesting in Othello, as characters that do the same thing are actually quite different. Think about how Othello and Iago both kill their wives. Same action, very different circumstances. Othello is misinformed and delusional. Iago, on the other hand, is cognizant and desperately trying to save face or inflict revenge. Same deal with Desdemona and Emilia: Desdemona lies to Othello about missing the handkerchief, but only because she doesn't want to hurt his feelings and is probably certain she'll find it soon anyway; Emilia, on the other hand, lies to Desdemona about the same handkerchief because she's a thief who put her husband before her friend. So it seems that, if we are to interpret actions as tools of characterization, Shakespeare is asking us to look a little beyond the action itself to the *motivation* behind it. This is where we get information about the characters. And that information (Iago is a villain, Othello is gullible, Desdemona is naïve, and Emilia just wants to be loved) is consistent with everything else we know.

Family Life

This tool of characterization gives us an opportunity to compare marriages. Othello has fallen deeply in love with Desdemona and married her because of that love. His marriage is new, and he is still getting used to giving up his independence to be with her. Iago, on the other hand, has been married to Emilia for a long time, and it's hard to see any love in their relationship. He seems tired of her, and only talks to her to insult her or to get her to do things for him. Cassio is unmarried and comes off as something of a playboy. He's not that into his girlfriend, Bianca, a prostitute who's obsessed with him, and is happier smooching the married Emilia.

Habits

Othello is extremely self-disciplined. He's obviously a favorite with the Duke, and deservedly so, it would seem, as he doesn't even protest when a call to war interrupts his honeymoon. Iago gets the job done, but he's always scheming behind the scenes – he uses his job as a screen for his machinations. Then we've got the story-telling habit: Othello tells true stories to Desdemona that make her fall in love with him, whereas Iago uses false stories to break up that very marriage. Again, these habits reveal the natures of the characters: Othello is genuine, Iago is not.

Occupation

Othello is the number one general of the entire Venetian fleet, and he rose to his position in Venice against all odds – he's the only black-skinned foreigner with a leading military position in Venice. Iago is one of Othello's back-up guys, and despite many years of experience as a soldier he is passed over for promotion. Cassio is Othello's new number-two guy, even though he's more of a brainy technical guy than a battle-ready warrior. This is an important point as it gives us some potential, or at least partial, motivation for Iago's bad behavior: he's jealous of Othello's success at work. In the same line of reasoning, we can see why Iago doesn't mind taking out Cassio along the way.

Sex and Love

Othello is passionately in love with Desdemona, but the way he views her sexuality shifts as Iago puts not-so-nice thoughts in his head. Othello is not inherently distrusting of women; rather, he is convinced to be so.

Let's face it, Iago's a pig—he claims all women are sex-obsessed and survive in the world by sleeping around. In his words, women "rise to play and go to bed to work" (2.1.4). Iago's ideas about female sexuality eventually rub off on Othello.

Speech and Dialogue
Othello, a Poetic Speaker
For a man who makes his living waging war, Othello's speech is consistently eloquent and strangely poetic. Stopping a group of men from getting into a fight, Othello calls out, "Keep up your bright swords, for the dew will rust them" (1.2.9).

Iago, a Man of All Tongues
Iago, in contrast, varies his speech according to the people who surround him. Often he is deceptively bland, his plain speech earning him the title of "honest Iago" even as he spins his web of lies and mwah-hah-hahs his way through life. At times, he is filthy with his language, as when he tells Desdemona's father that she and Othello are "making the beast with two backs." Again, he chooses to speak this way because it does the trick and gets the job of the hour done. But Iago's language is at his most masterful as he convinces Othello that Desdemona is cheating on him. Iago's lines are full of sudden stops, apologies, broken-off lines, as he delicately feigns reluctance to tell.

Cassio, a Man of Unremarkable Tongue
Unlike these two silver-tongued men, Cassio's speech is unremarkable. His only skill is in crafting pretty compliments for the ladies.

Desdemona, a Lady with Purpose
Desdemona's speech is full of passion and conviction. From the opening scene where she explains her love for Othello to a hostile audience, to her defense of her own innocence when her husband gets abusive and accusatory, Desdemona always speaks boldly and from the heart. She never hesitates to share her mind, and what she says is straightforward and eloquent.

Emilia, a Bitter Wife
Emilia, on the other hand, says little, and her speech only grows inspired when she is talking bitterly about the cruelties of men to women. Emilia's instinct, when Desdemona is being falsely accused, is to curse and look for someone to blame.

Literary Devices

Symbols, Imagery, Allegory

Handkerchief

The most dominant symbol in the play is the handkerchief that circulates throughout the play. Because Othello gave it to Desdemona as a first gift, the handkerchief functions as a token of his love, which Desdemona cherishes (3.3.1). This is why Iago convinces his wife to steal it from Desdemona – he knows that it has a lot of sentimental value and that Othello will be angry when he finds out his wife no longer has it.

Iago also knows that, for Othello, the handkerchief symbolizes Desdemona's fidelity. When it shows up in Cassio's possession, Othello is convinced that Desdemona is unfaithful. The white napkin, as we know, is spotted with red strawberries and Othello tells Desdemona that the strawberries were hand stitched with thread that has been dyed with blood from "maidens' hearts" or, virgins' blood (3.4.10). In this way, the handkerchief resembles a white wedding sheet that's also been stained with a virgin's blood. So, in Othello's mind, as long as Desdemona has the handkerchief in her possession, she's chaste. But, the moment she "loses it," she looses her chastity.

The handkerchief also seems to function as a symbol of Othello's mysterious past and his "exoticness." He tells Desdemona that an Egyptian "charmer" gave it to his mother and that it would keep his father "faithful" and under her spell (3.4.9). That such a small object has such enormous weight in the play testifies to the sensitivity of jealous minds, and the way that small incidents can be magnified psychologically into "proofs" of love or betrayal.

Honesty

You've probably noticed how the word "honest" shows up all over the place in *Othello*. By poet and literary critic William Empson's count, there are 52 uses of "honest" and "honesty" throughout the play. Like the word "nothing" in *King Lear*, "honest" has a wide range of meaning in *Othello*. At times, it refers to chastity, the question of whether a woman is "honest" or whether she is promiscuous. At other times, the word refers to personal honesty, whether or not a person is telling the truth. It can also refer to whether or not a person is a good and loving friend.

These meanings come together in some ironic ways throughout the play. The clearest example of this is how Iago uses personal dishonesty (lies and deceit) to convince Othello that his wife is sexually dishonest (cheating on her husband), all while pretending to be looking out for the best interests of his so-called friend. Check out how Iago plays the martyr when Othello warns him that he, Iago, better not be lying about Desdemona:

IAGO
O wretched fool.
That livest to make thine honesty a vice!

O monstrous world! Take note, take note, O world,
To be direct and honest is not safe.
I thank you for this profit; and from hence
I'll love no friend, sith love breeds such offence.
OTHELLO
Nay, stay: thou shouldst be honest.
IAGO
I should be wise, for honesty's a fool
And loses that it works for.
OTHELLO
By the world,
I think my wife be honest and think she is not; (3.3.52)

War

Every major character in the play packs up and heads for Cyprus, where we've been promised a bloody battle. And then, due to inclement weather, there is no war. We, the innocent and unknowing reader, accept this with a little confusion and move right into the sordid plot.

We might forget about the whole war thing until Othello's crucial monologue in Act 3, Scene 3, in which he describes the components of the battlefield – horses, troops, trumpets, banners, cannons – and how they are all lost to him now that he knows Desdemona is unfaithful. Here, these implements of war become symbols of Othello's sexuality. Think about it – what's more manly than a big collection of warlike objects? Desdemona has deflated him; he is un-manned by her betrayal.

So what's the conclusion? We got our war in Cyprus, after all; it's just that the battlefield turned out to be the mind, not the literal battlefield. If all is fair in love and in war, then it's a bloody battle indeed going on in Othello's psyche.

The Willow Song

As Desdemona is preparing for bed the night she will be murdered, she starts singing a song about willow trees. This song, supposedly sung originally by one of Desdemona's mother's servants who loved a crazy guy, reflects Desdemona's own situation. She herself is worried that the man she married has gone crazy and will desert her. Willows at the edge of water are a traditional symbol of women deserted by their lovers. (In another Shakespearean example, Ophelia, deserted by her love, Hamlet, dies after she falls out of a willow tree and drowns in a brook in the play *Hamlet*).

Cassio's Naughty Dream

Of course you're wondering about the naughty dream Cassio supposedly has one night. Before we discuss what's going on, let's recap, shall we?

IAGO
In sleep I heard him say 'Sweet Desdemona,
Let us be wary, let us hide our loves;'
And then, sir, would he gripe and wring my hand,
Cry 'O sweet creature!' and then kiss me hard,

As if he pluck'd up kisses by the roots
That grew upon my lips: then laid his leg
Over my thigh, and sigh'd, and kiss'd; and then
Cried 'Cursed fate that gave thee to the Moor!'
OTHELLO
O monstrous! Monstrous! (3.3.56)

When Othello asks for "living reason" (proof) that Desdemona's been "disloyal," Iago tells him about a sexy dream that Cassio supposedly had one night while he was lying in bed next to Iago (presumably, at an army camp). According to Iago, Cassio talked in his sleep while dreaming about a steamy encounter with Desdemona. Not only that, but Cassio also grabbed Iago, wrapped his leg over his thigh, and made out with him, all while dreaming about Desdemona, of course.

What's going on here? First, it's important to note that Iago is framing Cassio to make it look like he's sleeping with Desdemona. Second, Othello seems willing to accept this graphic story as "proof" that Desdemona's cheating. Third, Iago is describing a blatantly homoerotic moment he has allegedly shared with Cassio. The description of the dream is *supposed* to be about Desdemona and Cassio, but that becomes less important than the graphic description of what goes down between Cassio and Iago, which begs the following question: Is Othello upset/jealous that Cassio (allegedly) had dream about his wife, or that Cassio was lying in bed and groping *Iago*? Literary critics have argued both ways, so take your pick.

Gardens
Iago is pretty fond of making references to gardens and other kinds of foliage, wouldn't you say? The most famous moment in the play is when Iago says:

Our bodies are our gardens, to the which
our wills are gardeners: so that if we will plant
nettles, or sow lettuce [...] either to have it sterile
with idleness, or manured with industry, why,
the power and corrigible authority of this lies in our wills. (1.3.5)

This is a rather elaborate analogy between gardening and exercising free will. Basically, Iago is reminding us that he's the ultimate *master gardener*, so to speak, because he has such great control over himself and his actions. We're also reminded that, part of what makes Iago such a brilliant manipulator of Othello is his ability to *plant the seeds* of doubt and jealousy in Othello's mind.

Animals
We had a feeling you might check here for some ideas about all the animal references in the play. Check out our "Quotes on Race" for our thoughts on this, but come right back!

Candle
The candle that Othello blows out just before he strangles Desdemona symbolizes Desdemona's fragile life. Othello draws the comparison himself – as he stands over a sleeping Desdemona with a lit candle in his hand, he says he's going to "Put out the light, and then put

out the light" (blow out the candle and then strangle Desdemona). He also muses that the difference between Desdemona's life and a candle's light is that he can put out and relight the candle over and over if he so chooses, but he can kill Desdemona only once: "If I quench thee, thou flaming minister, / I can again thy former light restore, / should I repent me," he says to the candle. "But," he says to the sleeping Desdemona, "once put out thy light, / Thou cunning'st pattern of excelling nature, / I know not where is that Promethean heat / That can thy light relume" (5.2.1). Yep, that's pretty creepy.

Setting

Venice and Cyprus

The play starts in Venice and moves to Cyprus when the Turks invade.

Venice

Early modern (c. 1500-1750) Venice is a prosperous Italian city and a symbol of law and civilization. It's also full of white people, which makes Othello, a black Moor, stand out among the Venetians. (Check out our discussion of the theme of "Race" if you want to know about the implications of this.) Venice also happens to be renowned for its courtesans (prostitutes). When the English thought about Venice, they often imagined it to be a city full of promiscuous women. Now that's quite a coincidence, given that *Othello's* plot hinges on Othello's suspicions about his wife's fidelity, don't you think? Check out what Thomas Cory at has to say in his account of his travels to Venice:

[t]he name of a Courtesan of Venice is vamoosed over all Christendom [...] The woman that professeth this trade is called in the Italian tongue Cotezana, which word is derived from the Italian word cortesia that signifieth courtesie. Because these kinds of women are said to receive courtesies of their favorites [...] As for the number of these Venetian courtesans it is very great. For it is thought there are of them in the whole city and other adjacent places, as Murano, Malamocco, etc. at the least twenty thousand, whereof many are esteemed so loose that they are said to open their quivers to every arrow, a most ungodly thing without doubt that there should be tolleration of such licentious wantons in so glorious, so potent, so renowned a cit." (*Coryat's Crudities* , 1611)

Cyprus

Eventually, action moves to a military encampment in Cyprus, an island sacred to Venus, the goddess of love. On the island of love, away from civilization and rationality, all hell breaks loose and Iago is able to convince Othello that Desdemona has been cheating on him. At this military camp, Desdemona has lost any kind of support system she may have had in her hometown of Venice, so she's vulnerable to the kind of violence associated with the world of men and military.

Genre

Tragedy

The Tragedy of Othello, the Moor of Venice is a "tragedy" alright, and not just because the word "tragedy" appears in the play's title. We've got a handy list of the features and conventions that are so common in this genre, so let's take a look, shall we?

Dramatic work: Check. And by "Check," we mean that, yes, *Othello* is a "play."

Serious or somber theme: Hmm. *Othello*'s a study of the consequences of jealousy and racism, so check.

Hero's got a major flaw of character or conflict with some overpowering force: Check. You've probably picked up on the fact that Othello's a guy with a *serious* flaw (insane jealousy). Not only that, but Othello's also gullible – it doesn't take much for Iago to convince Othello that Desdemona's cheating on him (even though she's not). This, as some literary critics have argued, may have something to do with 1) Othello's suspicion that all women are inherently promiscuous and/or 2) Othello's fear that he, a black man, is not good enough for his white wife. Check out our theme discussions on "Race" and "Gender" for more on this.

Hero is destined for destruction and downfall: Check – sort of. The important thing to remember is that Othello experiences a major, major downfall over the course of the play. He starts out as a pretty noble guy – he's a celebrated war hero, he's obviously overcome quite a bit in order to reach the rank of a military general, he's respected by the Venetian government, he's a loving husband who has snagged a great wife, he's an eloquent storyteller (kind of like Shakespeare), and so on. By the end of the play, Othello's an irrational, violent, and insanely jealous husband who murders his own wife. Yet, while the idea of "destiny" plays an important role in plays like *Macbeth* and *Hamlet*, it's not really a factor in *Othello*. Some critics have argued that Othello's downfall is the "inevitable" outcome of Iago's masterful scheming and/or the racism Othello is subjected to in the play, but "destiny" doesn't seem to have much of a role here.

*Shakespearean tragedies always end in death but with some promise of continuity: Not all tragedies end in death, but all of *Shakespeare's* tragedies do. By the time we reach the end of the play, Othello has strangled Desdemona, Iago has killed Emilia, and Othello stabs himself in the guts. But, not everyone on stage is left for dead – Lodovico promises to return to Venice, where he will relate the tragic story of what has just happened to his countrymen. This is similar to what happens at the end of *Hamlet*, when Horatio promises the young prince that he will tell Hamlet's story to the world.

Othello's influence can also be seen in modern day psychological suspense thrillers (think writer James Patterson or film director Stanley Kubrick) because the entire momentum of the play is based on the twisted mind games of two (and often more) characters.

Tone

Cynical, Paranoid

The tone of *Othello* is dominated by Iago's voice. He is the only one in the play who speaks to the audience, and his bitter rants about Othello and Cassio, his casual dismissal of women as worthless prostitutes, and his gleeful self-congratulation about the nasty things he's doing are the foundation of how we view the story. Othello even starts to mirror Iago's bitter tone in his own rants about jealousy and sexual impurity.

Writing Style

Verse and Prose

Othello, like Shakespeare's other plays, is written in a combination of verse (poetry) and prose (how we talk every day). (Note: The play *Richard II* is the *one* exception to this rule – it's the only Shakespeare play written entirely in verse.)

Verse

Reading *Othello* often feels like reading a lengthy poem and that's because Shakespeare's characters often speak in verse.

What kind of verse do they speak? Well, the nobles typically speak in unrhymed "iambic pentameter" (also called "blank verse"). Don't let the fancy names intimidate you – it's pretty simple once you get the hang of it. Let's start with a definition of "Iambic Pentameter":

An "iamb" is an unaccented syllable followed by an accented one. "Penta" means "five," and "meter" refers to a regular rhythmic pattern. So "iambic pentameter" is a kind of *rhythmic pattern* that consist of *five iambs* per line. It's the most common rhythm in English poetry and sounds like five heartbeats: ba-DUM, ba-DUM, ba-DUM, ba-DUM, ba-DUM.

Let's try it out on this line from *Othello*:

FareWELL the TRANquil MIND, fareWELL conTENT

Every second syllable is accented, so this is classic iambic pentameter. When the lines have no rhyme scheme, we call it "Unrhymed Iambic Pentameter," which is also known as "Blank Verse."

Blank verse, as we've said, is typically reserved for the nobility and other important characters since it's kind of a formal way to speak.

Prose

Not everyone in the play speaks in blank verse, which we've established is the elegant, high-class way of talking. Characters lower on the social scale don't talk in a special poetic

rhythm; they just talk.

What's Up With the Title?

Today, we know the play as simply, *Othello*. But check out the title page of the 1622 quarto (the first published edition of the play): *The Tragedy of Othello, the Moor of Venice*. The full title not only suggests the play's about some guy named "Othello," it also alerts us to the fact that Othello's status as a black "Moor" in (a mostly white) "Venice," is going to be a pretty big deal in this play. Check out "Why Should I Care?" and our discussion of the theme of "Race" for more on this.

What's Up With the Ending?

We know that by the play's end Othello has transformed from a noble general and loving husband into a jealous, irrational killer. We also know that after Othello learns the truth (that he killed the ever-faithful Desdemona for no good reason), he decides to end his own life. Given the nature of the play's ending, it seems like Othello's final words are worth taking a close look at, don't you think? Here's what our protagonist says just before he stabs himself in the guts:

Soft you; a word or two before you go.
I have done the state some service, and they know't.
No more of that. I pray you, in your letters,
When you shall these unlucky deeds relate,
Speak of me as I am; nothing extenuate,
Nor set down aught in malice: then must you speak
Of one that loved not wisely but too well;
Of one not easily jealous, but being wrought
Perplex'd in the extreme; of one whose hand,
Like the base Indian, threw a pearl away
Richer than all his tribe; of one whose subdued eyes,
Albeit unused to the melting mood,
Drop tears as fast as the Arabian trees
Their medicinal gum. Set you down this;
And say besides, that in Aleppo once,
Where a malignant and a turban'd Turk
Beat a Venetian and traduced the state,
I took by the throat the circumcised dog,
And smote him, thus. (5.2.66)

Here, Othello says he "loved" Desdemona "too well" (too much), which suggests that he doesn't really understand the implications of what he's done.

Othello also seems pretty preoccupied with how people will think of him after his death. On the one hand, he wants to be remembered as a soldier who "has done the state some service" and who has killed a lot of Venice's enemies. Yet, he also seems to think that strangling Desdemona is a crime against the Venetian state – Othello compares himself to a "turban'd

Turk" (Venice's sworn enemy) which he emphasizes when he kills himself with the very same sword he used when he "smote" the "malignant" Turk on the battlefield.

By this point, Othello sees himself as a savage outsider (like a "Turk" or a "base Indian"), which is what characters like Brabantio have been calling him all along. In other words, Othello seems to have internalized the racist ideas that he has encountered in Venice. It also seems like Shakespeare is asking us to consider whether or not this is the inevitable outcome when a society tells a man over and over again that he's a "savage."

Did You Know?

Trivia

- Harvard philosopher, Stanley Cavell, pointed out that there is a "demon" in Des**demon**a and a "hell" in Ot**hell**o. (Source: Schalkwyk, David. *Speech and Performance in Shakespeare's Sonnets and Plays* . Cambridge, England; New York: Cambridge University Press, 2002. 195.)
- There have been several productions of Othello performed with all-black casts, and at least one, like a production in 1998 starring Patrick Stewart, in which Othello is white and the rest of the cast is black. (Source)
- In England in 1826, black actor Ira Aldridge became the first black man to actually play the role of Othello. Aldridge happened to be married to a white woman himself. (Source)
- In more recent years, one of the first well-known black actors to play Othello was Paul Robeson, a high-profile black actor, singer, and activist. Robeson played the title role in productions in England in 1930 and in the United States in 1943. These were groundbreaking productions (although not the first time a black actor played the role). (Source)
- For most of the play's performance history, Othello was played by a white actor in blackface (literally, a face painted black). That's how the role was played in Shakespeare's time. (Source)
- Ben Kingsley, who played Gandhi in the famous film Gandhi, has also played Othello. He portrayed Othello as a North African Arab. (Source)

Steaminess Rating

R

There's no sex on stage in *Othello* (and scholars debate whether or not Desdemona and Othello ever even consummate their marriage), but the entire play is preoccupied with, well, sex. Thanks to Iago, Othello's unfounded jealousy hinges on the idea that Desdemona has cheated on him, which leads Othello to strangle his wife…in her bed. The play is also chock-full

of erotic imagery, like the vivid description of Desdemona's handkerchief (a white napkin embroidered with red strawberries, which happen to be made with thread that's been dyed with virgin's blood), which is a visual stand-in for Desdemona's soiled wedding sheets. Iago even comes off as an aspiring pornographer when he describes a steamy dream Cassio supposedly had about Desdemona. Want more? Of course you do. Check out our "Quotes" for the theme of "Sex."

Best of the Web

Movie or TV Productions

Othello, 2001
http://imdb.com/title/tt0275577/
This made-for-TV movie turns *Othello* into a modern day crime story.

Othello, 1995
http://imdb.com/title/tt0114057/
Oliver Parkerdirects Laurence Fishburne as Othello, Kenneth Branagh as Iago, and Irene Jacob as Desdemona.

Othello, 1965
http://imdb.com/title/tt0059555/
Othello with Laurence Olivier as Othello, Frank Finlayas Iago, and Maggie Smithas Desdemona, directed by Stuart Burge. Nominated for four Academy Awards.

Othello, 1990
http://imdb.com/title/tt0357995/
Director Trevor Nunn's famous stage version of the play was also filmed for TV. Starring Ian McKellen as Iago, withWillard Whiteas Othello, andImogen Stubbs as Desdemona.

O, 2001
http://imdb.com/title/tt0184791/
O, a teen movie based on *Othello*, starring Mekhi Phifer as Othello, Julia Stiles as Desdemona, and Josh Hartnett as a heartthrob Iago. Set at a prestigious high school, the Othello character is the school's star basketball player, and Iago the coach's son who is jealous of his father's favoritism for "Odin."

Videos

Othello Rap
http://www.youtube.com/watch?v=UC-f0drvdmM
By the Reduced Shakespeare Company. Guess what they rhyme with "Othello"…

Iago Monologue
http://www.youtube.com/watch?v=V82rzXwvJKE&mode=related&search=
Iago's "How am I a villain" monologue, with Kenneth Branagh as Iago.

Willow Song
http://www.youtube.com/watch?v=4mlOCcp-a7s&mode=related&search=
Desdemona's willow song from the 1995 film.

Movie Clip
http://www.youtube.com/watch?v=rMXHrpiXbeo
Orson Welles in *Othello*.

Images
Playbill
http://www.realhistories.org.uk/uploads/images/othello.jpg
An old *Othello* playbill.

Websites
Performance History
http://www.rsc.org.uk/othello/about/stage.html
Performance history of the play from the Royal Shakespeare Company.

Othello Rap
http://www.pbs.org/wgbh/masterpiece/merchant/ei_shortest.html
Click on Yorick's skull on the right of the page to listen to the Othello rap.

Printed in Great Britain
by Amazon

17174318R20061